D0312230

I Tried to Change So You Don't Have To

I Tried to Change So You Don't Have To

TRUE LIFE LESSONS

LONI LOVE

WITH JEANNINE AMBER

hachette
BOOKS

New York

Hachette Go, an imprint of Hachette Books
Hachette Book Group
1290 Avenue of the Americas
New York, NY 10104
HachetteGo.com
Facebook.com/HachetteGo
Instagram.com/HachetteGo

First Edition: May 2020

Hachette Books is a division of Hachette Book Group, Inc.

The Hachette Go and Hachette Books name and logos are trademarks of Hachette Book Group, Inc.

The publisher is not responsible for websites (or their content) that are not owned by the publisher.

The Hachette Speakers Bureau provides a wide range of authors for speaking events. To find out more, go to www.hachettespeakersbureau.com or call (866) 376-6591.

Print book interior design by Marie Mundaca

Library of Congress Cataloging-in-Publication Data has been applied for.

ISBNs: 978-0-306-87372-0 (hardcover), 978-0-306-87374-4 (ebook)
Library of Congress Control Number: 2020930799

Printed in the United States of America

LSC-C

10 9 8 7 6 5 4 3 2 1

For Niko (and every girl who's been through tough times), work hard and keep laughing and everything will turn out fine.

CONTENTS

CONTENTS

AUTHOR'S NOTE

In reading this book you should remember that I am a comedian. (I am also a television host and actress and an electrical engineer.) This is my memoir and it tells you about my life. But it's a tale told by a comedian and I believe that this entitles me to a good number of liberties. I have reordered and combined events and people. And I changed a whole lot of names and identifying details. And I have exaggerated and made some things up altogether to (I hope), make you smile or even laugh. But I have not changed the reality of my life, where I came from, and how I got from there to where I am now.

INTRODUCTION

Don't you just love that feeling when something good happens and you get to say to yourself, "All my hard work has finally paid off." Like after a good divorce settlement or when you finally win ten dollars on a scratch-off after buying a lottery ticket every week for eighteen years.

For me, one of those moments happened on April 29, 2018, at the Pasadena Civic Center. Let me paint you a picture: I looked hot, decked out in a chic and glamorous chin-length wig I call my "Anna Wintour" and rocking a floor-length dress covered in all kinds of silver crystal and sequins. That heavy-ass gown weighed almost as much as I do.

I settled into my velvet chair in the cavernous auditorium and looked around. The room was filled with the biggest names in daytime television: Vanna White, Alex Trebek, Judge Judy, and the entire cast of *The Young and the Restless*. Rubbing shoulders with all those stars felt like an accomplishment on its own. But I was there as more than just a spectator. The event was the Daytime Emmy Awards show and I, along with the fabulous Adrienne Houghton, Jeannie Mai, and Tamera Mowry-Housley, had been nominated for our work cohosting the syndicated daytime talk show *The Real*. We'd only been on air five years, but we were up against three of the highest-rated talk shows on daytime TV: *The Talk, The View,* and *Live with Kelly and Ryan.*

Even though we worked our asses off to earn a seat at that table, we didn't think we had a shot at winning. We didn't have the big budget or the legacy of a show like *The View,* which has been a daytime staple for more than two decades. We couldn't afford to do lavish gift giveaways for our audiences, and we didn't book Hollywood's most coveted stars, like Tom Hanks or Denzel Washington. Not only that, we didn't look like the other shows, either. On *The Real* every host is a woman of color. We were the first and only daytime talk show without a white cohost. When we first hit the air, critics said we'd never last.

Chris Harrison, the host from *The Bachelor,* was presenting the Emmy for our category. Just like he does on *The Bachelor,* Chris served the award with extra drama. He leaned into the mic and announced the winner with a few excruciatingly well-timed pauses: "And the Emmy goes to... [pause]... the cohosts of... [pause]..." When he finally said *The Real,* I was so stunned that for a second I didn't move. Then I came to my senses, jumped from my seat, and bolted to the stage. I was determined to grab that award before somebody from the National Academy of Television Arts and Sciences jumped in and said they changed their minds.

If you'd been seated in the audience that night, you would have known immediately that we hadn't expected to win. The four of us were like a bunch of kittens running every which way.

While I was hightailing it to the front of the room, Adrienne was running in the other direction, toward our staff who were seated a few rows behind us. She wanted to give them all a hug. Meanwhile, Jeannie was taking off her shoes getting ready to sprint like a track star, and Tam was busy kissing her husband, Adam, which is why you should never go to an awards show with a date.

I was the first one to make it onstage. I clutched the golden statue—the same award that I'd seen Oprah Winfrey, Ellen DeGeneres, and Kelly Ripa win many times before—and looked out into the crowd. I had worked so hard for this moment of recognition. Despite the missteps and disappointments along the way—the failed auditions, the deals that went nowhere, the "big breaks" that fizzled into nothing—I'd finally arrived. As the rest of the girls leaped onstage to join me, I clutched our Emmy, savored the moment, and burst into tears.

I didn't get to Hollywood the way a lot of other people do. I wasn't a child star or the child of a star. I didn't write for a college humor magazine, study acting in New York, or know anyone in "the industry." In fact, until I was in my twenties, my idea of hitting the big time meant holding down a regular nine-to-five desk job, with benefits. Where I come from, having an employee dental plan meant you were living the dream.

I grew up in the Brewster-Douglass Housing Projects on the east side of Detroit during the height of the crack epidemic. Back then, it felt like there were two options for girls like me: I could be a drug dealer's girlfriend, or I could be the best friend of a drug dealer's girlfriend and hope I got an invite when he treated her to a Big Mac and fries. I didn't grow up with fantasies of having a glamorous life because around me all I saw was struggle. Maybe one day meeting Tito Jackson was as big as I dared to dream. But that doesn't mean I wasn't doing everything I could to improve my circumstances.

As a kid, I was always going the extra mile. When I joined the school orchestra in fourth grade and the music teacher told the class to each pick an instrument, I didn't run like the rest of the kids to sign up for the violin, oboe, or even the sassy triangle. I picked something big, bold, and beautiful: the French horn. And when I needed to make some extra money as a teenager to buy clothes for school, I didn't start selling drugs, even though opportunities were everywhere. Instead, I started a little grocery delivery service, making trips to the corner store for Brewster-Douglass senior citizens who needed a tin of Spam, a pack of Newports, or a tub of off-brand cottage cheese.

At Brewster-Douglass, I was the resident nerd, with my glasses and book bag, forever lugging around that big brass French horn. While other kids were hanging out on the corner listening to Kurtis Blow, I was the goody-two-shoes who lived for math club and didn't mess with boys. But the sad fact about living in the projects is sometimes no matter how hard you work, you still end up on the bottom. By the time I was seventeen years old, I was about as low as you can get: homeless and living out of my car. I remember crying my eyes out one night curled up in the front seat of my beat-up 1979 Chevy Chevette. I was miserable. And not just because I had to sleep with a gearshift sticking up my ass.

Of course, I am not the first person to face hardships.

Overcoming trials and tribulations is how we learn to get ahead. I've discovered that getting out of a bad situation is one part hard work, one part luck, and one part divine intervention. I'd been living in my car for more than a month when God stepped in and sent me an angel. Only this dude was disguised as a middle-aged man carrying a clipboard and dressed in a crisp button-down shirt, because God is funny like that.

My angel was named Mr. Arnold, and when I was feeling most hopeless, he was there with a guiding hand, showing me what was possible and setting me on a path to a better life. I went from living in my car to getting accepted into college. Ultimately, I made my way to California, where I started my comedy career. I figured if I could survive Brewster-Douglass, the crack epidemic, and being homeless, of course I could make it in LA.

That's when I discovered that getting ahead in Hollywood is a lot harder than getting out of the hood. Things are changing now, but when I moved to LA in the early 2000s, if you looked like me—tall, dark-skinned, and curvy—casting agents and execs weren't interested. They were looking for "talent" that was perky, blond, and wore a size 00, which I didn't even know was a size until I moved to California. It's like studio execs all fell in love with Heather Locklear when they were in middle school and their tastes never changed. The only jobs I was offered were for fried chicken commercials or to fill any role that called for a Jamaican accent. If I could do a Jamaican accent, I'd be rich right now.

For years, I scrambled to get my foot in the door. In the process, I endured a lot of criticism and rejection. My confidence got shaky and I began to lose my way. I would lie in bed at night and think about all the things that were "wrong" with me. I became convinced that the only way I would be successful was if I changed.

I know I'm not alone. I get tweets and DMs all the time from fans who tell me all the ways they are trying to transform into a "better" version of themselves. Maybe you have a plan for reinvention, too? Maybe you're trying to lose sixteen pounds, learning to "be more assertive," or finding a way to be less broke. But no one is born thinking *I'm not good enough.* Other people put those ideas in your head. If you really think about it, aren't self-improvement "goals" just a list of other people's criticisms—"You're too fat / too shy / too unemployed"— turned into a to-do list of things you need to "fix"? One day it occurred to me: *What if all the bad shit everybody says about you is wrong?*

After all, I got myself out of the projects by *not* doing what other people expected from me. At Brewster-Douglass, I picked up a French horn, joined the math club, and did my own thing. No matter how many times I got called a nerd— or worse—I didn't let it get to me. In the end, I didn't just survive, I thrived. So why, as an adult, was I suddenly listening to other people tell me how to get ahead? Maybe I didn't need to "improve"; maybe what I really needed was to find my way back to the Loni I was before I let the critics and self-doubt lead me astray. That's when my journey to happiness and success really began.

These days I am happy and humbled to say I'm living *my* dream. During the week, I host a TV show that gives millions of women a space to feel like they are heard, and on the weekends, I play comedy clubs around the country making people laugh. I even fulfilled my childhood fantasy by meeting Tito Jackson. Who says dreams don't come true?

It's not just my professional life that's turned out great. I also found real love with a man who doesn't expect me to serve him food *or* do acrobatics in bed. Yes, sis, they *do* exist.

I realize being on the other side of forty, unmarried, childless, and spending more nights in comedy clubs and hotel rooms than in my own bed might not be your idea of happiness, but it's the perfect life for me. And that's *exactly* my point. The key to success is knowing what *you* want, then figuring out how to get it without having to change who you are. It means standing in your truth and telling everybody else, "This me, get used to it."

I know there are millions of people out there who are struggling the way I did, trying to change who they are so they can have a better life. Honey, I'm here to tell you, if you're a grown-ass adult still trying to change, it's probably too late now.

Life is too short to waste any more of your precious time. Consider this book a shortcut to gaining the life lessons that took me years to find out, such as the road to happiness begins with embracing yourself, "flaws" and all; and sometimes God sends you a messenger in disguise; and, whatever you do, don't date men who sleep in bunk beds, especially if you got bad knees.

Most of all, I hope as you read this book you will learn from my mistakes and have a few laughs along the way. I tried to change so you don't have to.

CHAPTER 1

PROJECT WISE: LESSONS YOU DON'T LEARN IN SCHOOL

I learned everything I know about love, life, and getting ahead in one of the last places most people would ever want to live: the infamous Brewster-Douglass Housing Projects, on Detroit's down and dirty east side.

Unless you came up the way I did, you might not know much about project life. Maybe your idea of "the hood" comes from the movie *Precious* or a few grimy episodes of *Law & Order: SVU,* so you think project life is where all the boys become drug dealers and all the girls end up pregnant or working the pole. Well, I'm here to let you know you've been completely misinformed. Only *some* of the boys I grew up with turned to selling drugs. And only Porsche, Chardonnay, and Mercedes made their money twerking naked at LeRoy's Gentlemen's Club. But that was their parents' doing, if you ask me. If you want your daughter to land an office job, don't name her after a luxury vehicle or your favorite alcoholic beverage. Everybody knows job recruiters sort résumés into two piles: one for people they imagine would fit in at the office Christmas party and the other for candidates with names like "Alizé" or "BMW 600 Series." I don't make these rules; I'm just saying.

My experience growing up in the projects wasn't anything like you see on TV. Brewster-Douglass is where I learned the important life lessons that really shape a woman, like never count on a dainty girl to clean a fish; shower curtains are not doors; and sometimes a big girl needs a big horn to make her happy. I know these might not be the kind of inspirational tidbits you find in Hallmark cards, that's why I'm writing this book.

I was born more than three decades after the first low-rise townhouses of the Brewster-Douglass Projects were completed in 1942. Over that time, the projects, located just north of downtown Detroit, grew and grew, until eventually they occupied more than five city blocks and housed as many as ten thousand people. It's hard to imagine now, but back in the day folks clamored to live in Detroit public housing. That's because compared to the alternative, Brewster Homes were considered a giant step up.

Like a lot of black folks in the city, my family moved to Detroit from down South. My grandmother, Clara Bell, hailed from Alabama and brought my mama and her three sisters north sometime in the 1940s. Before the Brewster-Douglass homes were built, families like mine were forced to live in the worst part of town, in neighborhoods called Paradise Valley and Black Bottom. The houses were broke down and tore up. Some of them were little more than sheds, without electricity or running water. But as more and more families like mine fled the Jim Crow South looking for a better life in Detroit, the government decided it needed a place to put all these poor black folks. And so, the Brewster-Douglass Housing Projects were born. It was basically government-funded segregation, public housing designated just for African Americans. Even so, one lady who'd been living in the projects since the 1950s told me that when she moved in it felt like she'd died and gone to heaven. That's how much better Brewster-Douglass was than life in Black Bottom.

By the time I was living there, Brewster-Douglass was like a city unto itself, with a bunch of row houses, a couple of six-story buildings, and five fourteen-story high-rise towers. I lived on the top floor of building number 7 with my mama and my older brother, Bruce. Our place had two bedrooms, which makes it sound almost luxurious. In fact, it was tiny. If you sat in the kitchen, you could watch the thirteen-inch black-and-white TV in the living room without even squinting. Every Saturday morning, I'd sit on a vinyl-covered kitchen chair watching *The Jackson 5ive* and *Schoolhouse Rock!* cartoons, while my mama pressed my hair with a hot comb she heated up on the coils of our electric stove.

I only have one memory of my father, Nathan, who left our family when I was a baby. In my recollection, my father had come by the apartment to visit. I remember him having a thick handlebar mustache and big eyes like mine. He was making himself a bath and he said to me, "If you really want to get clean, you gotta put some bleach in the water." Don't ask me what he meant by that. All I know is him sharing his bathing habits sure didn't make me wish he was around more. As a kid, I had a lot of chores to take care of, including keeping the bathroom clean. The last thing I needed was some weird-ass dude using up all my cleaning supplies for his personal hygiene.

Just because my daddy wasn't around doesn't mean Mama had

closed up shop. She was young and vibrant, with smooth coco skin and baby-making hips. She worked long hours as a nurse's aide at St. John's Riverview Hospital, and I guess she figured she deserved some grown-woman fun. In fact, I'm pretty sure Mama's fun time is how I ended up calling some guy I barely knew "Uncle Chico."

Before he suddenly became part of the family, I'd only ever seen Uncle Chico repairing transmissions under a tree out behind the auto parts store. Then one morning, I saw him coming out of Mama's bedroom and she tells me he's my uncle. I wasn't the only kid with an uncle who came outta nowhere. At school, hardly any kids had their fathers living in the house. But there were plenty of uncles coming and going. One especially good-looking brother was "uncle" to damn near every kid in my class.

Looking back, it couldn't have been easy for Mama to date while raising two kids. I was well behaved around adults, but I had a mean side-eye, which I gave to any dude who set foot in our apartment. No grown-ass man wants to be eyeballed by a seven-year-old with thirty-two pigtails in her hair. As salty as I was, Mama's bigger problem came from my brother, Bruce.

Bruce was six years older than me, and he was what we called "slow." At least, that's what we called it back in the seventies. He wasn't dumb, but school was a challenge for him and he never seemed to pick up on basic social cues. Where Bruce really excelled was in telling the truth, even if it's the last thing you wanted to hear.

One time, while Mama was out at the corner store with Uncle Chico buying themselves a fifth of Gordon's gin, the phone rang and Bruce picked up. All I heard him say to the person on the other end of the line was, "Hello? Uh-huh…uh-huh…No, she ain't here.…Uh-huh…Uh-huh…" Then he hung up.

A little while later, Mama came in with Uncle Chico. At first, Bruce didn't say anything. He just sat there on the plastic-covered brown corduroy sofa watching *What's Happening!* until Mama asked directly: "Baby, did anybody call when I was out?" This was before cell phones and answering machines. Even if they had existed, Mama didn't have that kind of money. Bruce was her answering machine and her personal secretary.

"Yeah," he answered, not looking up from the TV.

"Did you take a message?" Mama asked.

"Uh-huh," Bruce replied.

Mama sighed. "Baby," she said patiently. "When somebody calls, you gotta take a message. Then you gotta give it to me."

"I took a message," said Bruce. "It was the dude from last night who called you."

I glanced over and caught Uncle Chico shoot Mama a look with his eyebrows raised so high on his forehead they seemed ready to fly right off his face. Mama stared straight ahead, like she was frozen in space. Bruce kept right on talking.

"The bald-headed dude," he continued. "You know, that guy who was here this morning. He sat right there." Bruce pointed at the kitchen table. "He smoked two Newports and when you was in the bathroom he farted and it smelled like ham."

"Damn it, Bruce!" Mama said. "That's enough."

But Bruce was on a roll. "Then when you came back from the bathroom, you asked if he wanted some cornflakes. And he said, 'Baby, all I want is some more of that sugar.'"

Even at seven I knew this wasn't a message you give Mama with Uncle Chico sitting right there. But that didn't stop Bruce.

"Then, you all went back in your room and turned the radio up real high and I couldn't hear my show," he continued, his eyes still glued to the TV. "When you came out, dude said you taste good."

Bruce turned to me. "Loni, you was here. Don't you remember?" I pretended I didn't hear him and opened the fridge to pour myself some Kool-Aid instead. Out of the corner of my eye I could see Mama clutching at her heart. Uncle Chico stormed out of the apartment, slamming the front door as he left. With my nose in the fridge, I tried not to laugh. There is nothing more hilarious than a mama getting busted by her very own child. That was the first time I realized just how funny life could be.

～

Life in the projects wasn't always easy. Brewster-Douglass was filled with roaches and winos and all the elevators smelled like piss. The one place I loved was school. I loved the smell of magic markers, the gummy pizza we had every Friday for free lunch, and the way a cloud of chalk dust blew up when the teachers clapped their blackboard erasers together at the end of the day. I loved Miss Thompson, my first-grade teacher who turned me on to Dr. Seuss, and my third-grade teacher, Mrs. Carter, who showed me how to glide my pencil across the page in looping cursive script.

School is also where I discovered my love of classical music, in Mr. Shelby's orchestra class. Back then, even poor kids got music lessons at school. By fourth grade, we were allowed to choose our own instrument. I considered the triangle, but decided it was too prissy; then I thought about drums, but they were too loud. All it took was one look at that long, black clarinet to know the instrument was a hard pass for me. And then I saw her, the big, bold, and beautiful French horn calling my name. I loved her curves and shimmer and the way her sound made you stand up and take notice.

We were allowed to bring our instruments home to practice. Every day after I finished my chores, it was just me in the apartment playing scales over and over until I got them right. That's the advantage of being a latchkey kid: there was no one home to tell me to shut the hell up. While other kids were hanging out and getting into trouble, I was getting lost in Mozart's "Horn Concerto Number 4 in E Flat Major." All through high school, music was my escape. But as much as I thrived in school, my brother Bruce struggled.

One afternoon, Mama came home early and mad as hell. "Loni," she barked, "get your coat on." She called to Bruce, who was glued to the TV. "Baby, put on your shoes," she said. "You two are coming with me."

While my brother and I scrambled to get dressed, Mama scanned the apartment. Her eyes landed on my copy of *Green Eggs and Ham,* which was lying facedown on the kitchen table. She picked up the book, shoved it in her purse, and the three of us marched five blocks to Foster Elementary.

"Baby, keep up," Mama called over her shoulder to Bruce as we speed-walked through the school corridors to the principal's office. Mama had dragged us there to lodge a complaint. She'd gotten our report cards the day before and learned that Bruce had passed the eighth grade and had been promoted into high school. Mama was furious.

In the principal's office, Bruce and I stood silently behind our mother as she pled her case. "You keep promoting this child and he don't know how to read!" she said, motioning to Bruce.

"Ma'am," the principal interjected. "He's advancing to high school...that's a good thing!"

Mama reached into her purse and flung the Dr. Seuss book in Bruce's direction. "Baby, show this man how you read." My brother glanced at the book, then at our mother, without saying a word. "Show him," Mama urged. "Show the man what you know."

Bruce pointed to the words on the page. "Wooo...ud," he said tentatively, his brow furrowed in concentration. "Would you...l..."

"See?" my mama said, throwing up her hands. "What'd I tell you? You keep passing him, but you're not teaching him nothing." She snatched the book from my brother and handed it to me. "Loni, read the book," she demanded.

I cleared my throat dramatically: "I do not like green eggs and ham. I do not like them, Sam-I-am..."

Mama cut me off. "See? My daughter reads better than my son," Mama said to the principal. "And she's only in first grade." She put her hands on her hips. "Sir, my son needs more help."

My mother wasn't an educated woman and she certainly wasn't raised to believe she deserved any kind of special treatment. But she sure as hell wasn't about to let her son fall through the cracks. After that, Bruce got transferred to a special school. At night, Mama would help him with his homework. She told me, "Your brother needs special attention. But you're going to be okay." I took that to mean, "You're on your own, kid. You can take care of yourself."

For a long time, I was mad at my mama for thinking that as a child I had everything under control. But it turns out that when you're forced to fend for yourself, you find your hidden talents.

⌒

They don't tell you this in fashion magazines, but sometimes it pays to be bigger than everyone else. I should know. Starting from my very first day of school, I was the tallest girl in my class. Sure, it wasn't easy finding little kids' school shoes in a men's size 13. But my height gave me a hidden advantage. I first noticed it in second grade, when I had Miss Kilpatrick as a teacher. Miss Kilpatrick was a tiny woman with a very high-pitched voice and a very bad lisp. She had that ageless black-don't-crack smooth-skin beauty that made it impossible to tell how old she was. She might have been a young-looking forty-five-year-old. Or she could have been twelve. Either way, I was so tall and she was so petite that the two of us were practically eye to eye. Instead of treating me like a child, Miss Kilpatrick treated me like her assistant. I guess she assumed that because we wore the same dress size, I was practically an adult.

Most days, Miss Kilpatrick asked me to help her with the classroom chores, like cleaning the chalkboard and distributing spelling handouts to the class. But one day, a girl named Mavis French got a nosebleed after my best friend Peaches Lee clocked her for using all the glue stick. Miss Kilpatrick rushed over to Mavis, insisting she had to take her to the nurse's office. "Now, you children behave yourself while I'm gone," she said. Then she turned to me. "Loni, keep an eye on things. You're in charge."

What the hell? How was I supposed to know how to control a bunch of badass kids? I was only eight years old. These kids were going to tear me apart.

Standing at the front of the room after Miss Kilpatrick was gone, I could see kids beginning to fidget in their seats. My classmates were the type of kids to fling a teacher's desk out the window if nobody stopped them. I figured I had about eight seconds before the class descended into total mayhem; I had to act fast.

"Okay, everybody," I said in my loudest voice. "Settle down." Everybody ignored me. "I mean it, class," I repeated, "settle down!" Only this time I said it with an exaggerated lisp, doing my best Miss Kilpatrick impression. "I mean it, claTH. THettle down!" Peaches, who was sitting in the front row, giggled.

"Thettle down, claTH!" I said again, louder. "Or I'm gonna get THO mad!"

From the corner of my eye, I could see my crush, Willy Williams, banging his fist on his desk in appreciation. "Yo, girl, you funny as shit," he said.

"Willy!" I yelled in his direction. "No curTHing in claTH!"

You don't know a tough crowd until you've had to entertain a bunch of Brewster-Douglass-raised second graders. But somehow, I kept the class laughing until Miss Kilpatrick came back. That is how I learned a very important life lesson: if someone thinks you're up to the job, they just might be right.

If I hadn't been able to control the room with my jokes, Miss Kilpatrick would have come back to her classroom to find a missing desk and possibly a few fatalities. Instead, she was so pleased that all the kids were in their seats and still breathing that she kept putting me in charge whenever she left the room.

I told so many jokes that year, by the time I moved on to third grade, I had a solid seven-and-a-half-minute set.

$$\backsim$$

I cut my teeth as an entertainer doing stand-up in Miss Kilpatrick's second-grade class. But by third grade, I'd gotten so confident I decided to share my talent with the world. To me, that meant performing at the annual Junior Talent Show, taking place in the auditorium at the Brewster-Wheeler Recreation Center, not far from where I lived. For my act, I decided to lip-sync to Deniece Williams's "Free." I practiced for days, playing Mama's worn record over and over on her little record player in the living room until I'd memorized all the words.

I was too young to understand the song's sexual undertones, but I'd watched enough *Soul Train*—and our local bootleg version called *The Scene*—to know that a musical performance was nothing without some kind of slick dance moves. So, I practiced those, too. Unfortunately, I was not at all what you would call coordinated. In fact, I was that rare black girl who really can't dance. But what I lacked in skills I made up for with attitude.

The night of the show, I got all decked out in my green-and-yellow plaid matching vest and capri pants set that my mother bought at Lucille's secondhand store and sashayed onto the stage, throwing my hands in the air like Diana Ross in the poster for *The Wiz*. Even though "Free" is a slow-tempo ballad, I rolled my little hips and tried to do some Temptations-style footwork. The audience, who was mostly mamas and a few "uncles" from the neighborhood, ate it up. Or maybe they thought I was having a seizure. Either way, by the time I finished, folks were up and out of their folding chairs giving me a standing ovation.

The excitement I felt that night was like nothing I'd ever experienced before. It felt like a million firecrackers had exploded in my belly and rained glitter and confetti all over my soul. More than a decade would pass before I got a chance to catch that same thrill. But I never forgot the feeling.

I have a theory that says the answer to all our most pressing questions—like, What should I do with my life?—can be found in our earliest memories. For instance, the more I think about it, the more convinced I am that I became a comic because, for my entire adult life, I've been chasing that Junior Talent Show high.

The Brewster-Wheeler Rec Center was the center of my universe. It's where I discovered my passion for entertaining and it's where I saw my second-grade crush, Willy Williams, burst into tears after missing a free throw in the gym. I'd never seen a boy cry like that before. In the projects, as soon as a boy is fresh out of diapers he's expected to man up. Willy got clowned for throwing an airball and for showing all that emotion. But it just made my crush grow stronger; I love a sensitive guy.

Most important, the rec center is also where I became a Girl Scout, which is how I learned my most important childhood lessons of all. A few months after my talent show victory, Miss French, who lived in building number 6 with her twin daughters, Mavis and Marvell, posted a flyer in the rec center announcing she was putting together a Girl Scouts troop.

Troop number 772 was some of the baddest Girl Scouts you'd ever want to see. And by "bad" I mean good. We killed it at community service, picking up trash, painting over graffiti, and cleaning up the rec center every Friday after school. Miss French had us working so hard, I wouldn't be surprised if she low-key had a cleaning contract with the city and was using us as child labor. We also sold the shit out of those damn cookies. Girl Scouts was some of the hardest work I've ever done in all my life. It was totally worth it, though, because Girl Scouts is how I got to go to summer camp.

Every summer, the girls in Troop 772 would pile onto a yellow school bus, armed with plastic shopping bags stuffed with clothes, toothbrushes, and faded blankets we'd grabbed from our beds at home, to spend one happy week away from the projects. Before summer camp, everything I knew about the world was what I learned at Brewster-Douglass, Foster Elementary, and the rec center. Summer camp was a game-changer. It was the first time I became aware that not every kid grew up like me.

Girl Scouts camp attracted troops from all over the city of Detroit and the surrounding suburbs, including places I didn't know existed, where kids lived in houses instead of apartment buildings and the dads came home every night. As soon as I saw the other girls step off their buses, I knew they were different. First of all, some of them were white. Back then, the only white people I knew were the Brady bunch, the Partridge family, and Mr. Shelby, my music teacher. Suddenly, here were white girls up close and personal, with all their freckles and straight blond hair. A few of them even had braces. What shocked me even more than seeing all those Cindy Bradys was the sight of two black girls stepping off the same bus.

The first black girl I noticed was Lauryn. She was put together in a way I'd never seen a kid look before. Imagine all the elegance of Diahann Carroll's Dominique Deveraux packed into the body of an eleven-year-old kid.

Lauryn's Girl Scout uniform was crisply starched, and her hair was slicked back into a single high pony, tied with a ribbon the exact same shade as our outfits. The way her edges were laid, she looked like she belonged on the cover of a box of Dark and Lovely hair relaxer.

I instinctively reached up and touched my own hair. The night before, my mother had taken three hours to wash, dry, and press my hair. She'd parted it carefully and braided it into four plaits, which she secured with mismatched plastic barrettes. But it was all for nothing. I'd been in nature less than an hour, but already all sorts of twigs and leaves had managed to get stuck up in my hair. I moved my hand and a small bird flew out.

Lauryn's younger sister Charlotte was my age but carried herself with the same air of sophistication. Not only did the girls speak like my third-grade teacher, Mrs. Wilkens—saying "Excuse me?" when they didn't hear something, instead of "Say what?" like the rest of us—but the sisters had also come to camp *accessorized*. Dangling from their ears were small but expensive-looking gold hoops, and Lauryn had a thin gold chain with a heart-shaped charm on her wrist. Plus, I noticed, she kept reapplying shiny lip gloss that smelled like cherry soda, which struck me as some next-level fancy shit. I was so fascinated by the sisters that on the first day, while we were all putting bait on our fishing hooks, I tried to strike up a conversation with Lauryn.

"What do they call you?" I asked. I'd never heard the name

Lauryn before. I assumed she went by a nickname, like every other kid I knew. "They call you L? Little L? Big L? Black L? Sassy L? Lo? La? Lola? Ryn? Ro? Ra-Ra? Lo-Ra?...Or what?"

"My name is Lauryn," she said flatly. And that was the end of our getting-to-know-you talk. I don't want to say the sisters were stuck-up, but I got the distinct impression that they were going out of their way to keep their distance from our troop. Almost like they thought being poor was contagious.

Even so, watching the sisters descend the steps of that yellow bus looking fly as hell, I couldn't help but feel a twinge of jealousy. I wanted a gold chain, laid edges, and ribbons that matched my outfit. I mean, who wouldn't? But all that jealousy quickly evaporated as soon as I realized these dainty-ass girls couldn't do shit. Lauryn and Charlotte were afraid of insects and terrified of the dark. They didn't know how to bait a line or scale a fish. And neither they, nor any of their little white friends, could figure out how the hell to pitch a damn tent.

I may have grown up in the projects, but I had no problem roughing it in the wild. I was used to going to the bathroom in the dark because our lights got turned off whenever Mama couldn't pay the electric bill, which was often. And the projects are the birthplace of all cockroaches in America, so of course I wasn't afraid of bugs. My grandma Clara Bell used to take me fishing for trout in the Detroit River, so I also knew how to slice a fish from head to tail, pull out the bones, flip it over, and scrape off the scales without squealing like the babysitter in a horror movie.

The only thing I didn't already know how to do when I got to camp was pitch a tent. But it turns out Brewster-Douglass had prepared me for tent life, too. Thanks to my mother's attempts at home renovation, I had learned how to ghetto MacGyver the shit out of any type of situation.

For instance, at home, Bruce and I shared a bedroom. One day, Mama got it in her head to rig up an old clothesline and hang a shower curtain across the middle of the room to give us some privacy.

"Look," she said brightly, gesturing to the plastic curtain with a Vanna White wave of her hand. "Now you each got your own rooms!"

A few hours later, in the dead of night, that shower curtain came crashing down harder than a junkie after a five-dollar hit. Hearing the commotion, Mama busted into our room wielding an old baseball bat and scaring me half to death.

The next night I took matters into my own hands. I got an extra-long extension cord and tied one end to the radiator. Then I got up on a chair, ran the line through the light fixture, around the top hinge on the door, and across the room. Balancing on top of the dresser, I tied the other end tightly around the metal clothes rod in the closet and secured the whole thing with a double half-hitch knot. In other words, when I got to summer camp I already knew the basics of suspension engineering. It wasn't that hard to figure out how to pitch a damn tent.

By the end of my week at Girl Scouts camp, I felt sorry for Lauryn and Charlotte and all their helpless little friends. They had come to camp with all kinds of luxuries, like Disney princesses sleeping bags and towels that matched their swimsuits. But if you left them alone in the woods—or the projects— they'd never make it out alive.

Growing up in Brewster-Douglass, I learned that making

folks laugh could save my ass and that having nice things is not as valuable as being resourceful. More than anything, I learned that everybody needs something that makes them feel like they can get away from all their troubles. I found peace and happiness practicing scales on my big-ass French horn and spending a hot summer week outside the city. I didn't know it at the time, but a few years later all around me folks in Brewster-Douglass would be finding another way to escape— one that took them out of the red-brick high-rises of the projects and straight into hell.

Brewster-Douglass Survival Guide

- Run first, ask questions later.
- Toilet paper can be used as a napkin, sponge, or maxi pad.
- You can fix anything with duct tape or Vicks VapoRub.
- There is more than one way to start a car with a screwdriver.
- You don't need shampoo, bubble bath, or shower gel. Use the damn dish soap by the sink.
- One cup Cheetos + ½ cup ketchup + two cups grated government cheese = lasagna.

CHAPTER 2

GOOD PEOPLE AND ONE BAD SANTA

"That's Satan's music," Mrs. Brooks said as we walked across the asphalt courtyard that ran through the center of the projects. It was early fall, and some of the older residents had dragged folding chairs outside onto the concrete slabs in front of their buildings to enjoy the last days of warm weather. A few of them had their transistor radios tuned to WJLB, the best R & B station in town. From every direction, I could hear the strains of Al Green begging, "Let's stay together..."

"You hear me, Loni?" Mrs. Brooks said. "The radio plays nothing but music about sin and fornication. It's nothing you should be listening to. Satan has his hands all over that soul music!"

This was news to me. If Al Green was sending secret devil messages in song, I wondered what Mrs. Brooks might think of the record my mama had brought home the other day—the cover of the Ohio Players' *Pain* featured a beautiful bald woman dressed in a studded black leather bikini and holding a whip. I opened my mouth to ask, but before I could even get the words out Mrs. Brooks had stopped in her tracks, closed her eyes, and begun to recite Scripture: "Let sexual immorality and every sort of uncleanness or greediness not even be mentioned among you!" She added: "It's right there in the Bible, Loni. Ephesians 5:3." Then she grabbed me by my hand and continued to pull me along.

Mrs. Brooks, who had long gray hair she braided in a thick plait and pinned into a bun at the nape of her neck, lived a few buildings over from us. She was a devout Jehovah's Witness and my after-school babysitter.

In the 1970s, there were a lot of programs to help low-income single parents like my mother afford childcare so they could get out and work. At least, I think that's what was going on. All my mama ever told me was "the government" paid for Mrs. Brooks's babysitting service. I had my suspicions, though. The way Mrs. Brooks had me hustling from door to door with her as she did her witnessing every afternoon, it was also possible that this old lady was paying Mama to use me as her personal assistant. Whenever we went out, Mrs. Brooks made me hold a grocery bag bulging with copies of the Jehovah's Witness magazines, *The Watchtower* and *Awake!* She was on a mission to show people the truth, which she insisted was contained in their pages.

As far as I could tell, most folks weren't interested. They would open the door, see Mrs. Brooks standing there—with her threadbare coat, sensible shoes, and holding a copy of *The Watchtower*—and shut the door in her face. If someone did let us in, it was almost always a woman. Even before they said a word, I could see in their eyes how desperate or sad or lonely they were. They just wanted someone to talk to.

Mrs. Brooks would lead me into their living rooms and sit me in front of a TV while she witnessed. Sometimes, I'd over-hear little bits and pieces of the conversations. One lady told Mrs. Brooks she'd lost her faith in God when her son was shot and killed, another started crying about her husband who had run off. In building 6, a middle-aged woman in a faded pink housedress eagerly invited us inside, but all she wanted was to know if Mrs. Brooks could catch her up on what was going on with the Roger–Holly–Janet love triangle on *Guiding Light*.

No matter how crazy the person seemed, Mrs. Brooks was always patient and kind. The only time I saw her turn away from her mission to spread the good news of the Kingdom was when a man in building 4 opened the door wearing a stained under-shirt, dirty sneakers, and no pants. He was holding an almost empty forty-ounce bottle of Olde English Malt Liquor.

"Church lady!" he said, laughing like a lunatic. "I bet you want some a dis!" He pointed to his crotch and gyrated his hips. Only then did he glance down and see me standing there. I was transfixed, frozen in the hallway with my jaw on the ground. I had never seen a grown man's ding-a-ling before.

"C'mon now!" he yelled drunkenly at Mrs. Brooks. "How you gonna show up here with a little kid? That ain't right, church lady!"

"Don't pay him no mind, Loni," Mrs. Brooks said, grabbing me by the hand and pulling me away. "The devil made him do it."

My mama never talked to me about religion, and I don't remember her ever taking me or my brother Bruce to church, not even on Christmas. So, Mrs. Brooks had a blank slate when it came to my religious instruction, and she went all in. She taught me that Armageddon was coming, any day now, and that only the righteous would live on in paradise on earth. She explained Scripture and lectured me on leading a moral and virtuous life, which she said meant no lying, no stealing, and definitely no fornication. She didn't go into detail about what fornication entailed, but from what I could tell it had something to do with holding hands and listening to Barry White.

"Loni," Mrs. Brooks said, "Satan will try to lead you astray, mark my words. But you hold firm, you hear me? You stay away from loose behavior and unclean thoughts."

I was seven years old.

On Sundays and Wednesdays, I would accompany Mrs. Brooks to her meetings at the Kingdom Hall, a sparsely decorated building on the west side of town. Kingdom Hall didn't look anything like any of the churches I saw on TV. There were no wooden pews or pretty stained-glass windows. There wasn't even a giant cross. Instead, the fluorescent-lit room had rows of folding chairs and an old guy at the podium leading us in Bible study. Sometimes we'd sing Jehovah's Witness music from a songbook called *Singing and Accompanying Yourselves with Music in Your Hearts.* There was never a choir or an organist at those meetings, either. The congregation raised their voices along to a record. Mrs. Brooks always sang the loudest in her old and warbling voice.

Mrs. Brooks was the most devout person I have ever known. She didn't just talk the talk, she also led by example, showing me what it looks like to move through the world with grace and generosity. You never forget the first person who teaches you how to be kind. To this day, I try to follow Mrs. Brooks's example and do my best to care for people in crisis, even when they aren't wearing any pants.

❀

Even though Mama had government help paying for Mrs. Brooks's babysitting-slash-proselytizing service, somehow we were still poor as hell. I'm not talking about skip-the-yearly-vacation or cut-back-on-Starbucks broke. I mean the kind of poor where you open the fridge and there's nothing on the shelves but a bottle of off-brand ketchup and half a loaf of day-old bread—and that's what's for dinner. We were so broke that Mama used to buy giant ten-pound sacks of potatoes, cook them up a bunch of different ways, and tell us those potatoes counted as a side, a vegetable, and a meat.

One Christmas, Mama sat me and Bruce down and told us that the hospital where she worked as a nurse's assistant had cut back on her hours. "Money is real tight right now," she said. "I don't have enough for Christmas dinner *and* presents for you kids. I can't cover both."

My eyes grew wide: "We're not gonna eat?"

"No, Loni," Mama corrected me. "We *are* gonna eat. I already bought a nice turkey for Christmas dinner. But there's nothing left for presents. You'll get something next year."

No presents? I was crushed. I had been busting my ass trying to be a good girl for months! I'd behaved myself at school and always did my after-school chores, including making dinner before Mama came home from work every night. When Mama invited her friends over for Friday night get-togethers, I was the one who emptied the ashtrays, swept the carpet, and picked up the empty beer bottles littering the living room on Saturday morning. Mrs. Brooks told me that Jehovah's Witnesses do not celebrate Christmas, which she called "a party for Satan." But I didn't care. I knew I deserved some damn presents.

More than anything, I wanted a Barbie doll—and not one of those cheap-ass fake Barbies they sold at the corner store, either. I wanted a Deluxe Quick Curl Barbie who came dressed in an evening gown and white fur shawl. I also wanted a Ken doll, a Barbie DreamHouse, and a miniature luxury toy sailboat, so Barbie and Ken could enjoy their glamorous doll lifestyle together. If I couldn't get Barbie and Ken and all their possessions, I'd settle for a Betty Crocker Easy-Bake Oven. And if not that, I'd take a Mr. Potato Head. With all those potatoes Mama made me eat, it was the least she could do.

It turned out Mama wasn't interested in me or my happiness. She didn't care about my presents at all. That's how I ended up that sad Christmas Day sitting with Mama and Bruce in our little apartment listening to gospel on the radio with not a single present in sight.

I was curled up on the end of the living room sofa thinking about Barbie and Ken and how happy the three of us would have been together, when suddenly I heard a knock at the front door and a man's deep voice on the other side calling, "Merry Christmas!"

My heart skipped a beat. *Oh my God! Santa is here!* I thought. *My prayers have been answered!*

From the hallway, Santa called my mother's name. "Frances!" he hollered. "Open the goddamn door!"

Before my mother could answer, I jumped up and bolted to the door. I flung it open and gasped in amazement at the man who stood before me. I couldn't believe my eyes; not only was Santa Claus black, he also had a Jheri curl!

"Oh, hey there, little lady!" Santa said. He sounded surprised to see me.

"Santa!" I yelled, grabbing him by the waist and hugging him. "You came!"

"Yeah, that's right," Santa chuckled. "Ho ho ho!" Then Santa walked right past me, making a beeline for my brother, who was sitting on the sofa leafing through a worn Superman comic book. "Hey, little man," Santa said. "How you doin'?"

Bruce looked up at Santa. Then at Mama. She sighed and pushed a strand of hair out of her face.

"Baby," she said to Bruce, "say hello to your daddy. He came to see you for the holiday. Ain't that nice?"

My eyes grew wide as saucers. "You had a baby with Santa?" I asked, amazed.

"Loni, he ain't Santa," my mother said with a sign. "This here is *Carl,* Bruce's daddy."

Wait . . . what? This was too much for my little kid brain to handle. Until that day, I thought Bruce and I had the same no-good dad. Now I was learning that not only did we each have our own father who never came around, but also my brother's dad was a Santa impersonator. *What in the name of Black Baby Jesus was going on?*

"I been away for a while," Fake Santa said offhandedly, as though that explained everything. "Loni, girl, last time I saw you, you was barely walking. Now look at you! You all big and shit. And, Bruce, my man!" he said turning to my brother. "What are you, like, eight, nine this year?"

"He's thirteen," said Mama flatly.

"I'll be fourteen in June," Bruce chimed in.

"Get outta town!" said Fake Santa. "I guess it's been a minute! But that's okay because I brought you some good shit, son. You gonna be real happy."

Fake Santa sat himself down on the sofa and looked around. He turned to my mother: "What, you ain't got no tree, Frances?"

Mama crossed her arms and ignored the question. Santa ignored Mama ignoring him. "Can't have a real Christmas without no damn tree," he muttered. "They come in silver now, real festive-looking. Them shits last forever." He turned his attention to Bruce. "Look here, son," he said. "Look what I got you."

As I watched from the sidelines, Fake Santa reached into the shopping bag and pulled out a brand-new GI Joe with Kung Fu Grip action figure: "You like this?"

Bruce shrugged.

"I knew you would!" Santa said. He reached back into the bag and pulled out an Evel Knievel Formula 1 Dragster toy car with a seven-inch Evel sitting in the driver's seat and handed it to Bruce. Then out came the Hot Wheels—a bright red fire truck, a tiny white ambulance, and a yellow Hot Fire racer.

I thought for sure Fake Santa was done, but the presents kept on coming. Fake Santa gave Bruce a Magic 8 Ball, a pair of Lee jeans, two packs of white tube socks with stripes, and a green turtleneck sweater two sizes too small. When he was done, Bruce was left standing in a pile of discarded plastic wrap and cellophane packaging, his arms bursting with clothes and toys. Meanwhile, I had nothing: no Barbie, no Ken, and definitely not Barbie's beautiful DreamHouse or her doll-sized sailboat. I didn't even have a crappy Mr. Potato Head.

I sucked in my breath and blinked hard, trying not to cry. But it was a losing battle. My shoulders heaved as tears and snot ran down my face.

Mama reached over and pulled me close. "Carl, you didn't think to bring a little something for Loni?"

Fake Santa shot me a look of surprise, like he just noticed I was in the room and wasn't sure how I got there. "Hey, hey," he said. "Don't cry, now." He grabbed a package out of Bruce's hands. "This is for you. Look! See, these are fresh to death! You gonna look real nice in these."

He shoved the package at me: a set of boys' plain white undershirts, size 8 to 10. They didn't even have a design on them. I held them to my chest and sobbed even louder.

"This ain't right, Carl," Mama said. "This ain't right at all." I looked up at my mother. She was crying, too.

I'm sure every kid raised by a single parent has a story about a Christmas or birthday disappointment. You know, the stories where they are sitting by the window for hours waiting for some deadbeat who never shows up. The details don't matter. It's the hurt feelings you never forget. All these years later, every time I think about those damn boys' undershirts, I get choked up.

People won't tell you this, but sometimes when you feel let down by some asshole who forgot your birthday—or by a shitty Fake Santa who didn't bring you a gift—it's actually a *good* thing. It means you expect people to do better. Thanks to Mrs. Brooks, even as a seven-year-old I knew what kindness and care looked like. That little old lady walked door-to-door for hours on end—through rain, sleet, and snow like a damn postal worker!— all so she could save a few souls. But this dumb-ass Fake Santa couldn't even spend five minutes thinking about me. I couldn't put it into words at the time, but I realize now I felt hurt because deep down I knew I deserved to be treated better than this.

As sad as Christmas was that year, I learned two important life lessons that day. Number one: Feeling let down by someone's bad behavior is a healthy sign that you know your worth. And number two: If Santa shows up with a Jheri curl, don't let him in.

Poor Folks' Santa Claus

The sad fact is that Santa is not an equal opportunity gift giver. He only brings bicycles, iPhones, and designer clothes to kids in certain parts of town. If you live in the hood, you quickly learn that Santa has a whole different sack of toys he's reserved just for you. You know you're broke when Saint Nick gives you this for Christmas:

- A pack of shoelaces with a note, "You'll get the kicks next year"
- A McDonald's Happy Meal box filled with ketchup packs, napkins, and a bologna sandwich
- Your big brother's clothes wrapped in gift paper
- A "doctor's kit" made from Band-Aids and plastic vials that look just like the ones in the alley behind the playground
- A pack of frozen chicken thighs
- A personalized ankle monitor
- A can of Spam with a bow on top
- A homemade card with five dollars in food stamps inside
- A carton of Newports
- A toy that you swear went missing from your room last week

CHAPTER 3

MY LIFE OF CRIME

Like a lot of kids at Foster Elementary, I got free lunch at school. On Mondays, we had gray hamburger patties that tasted like Styrofoam; on Tuesdays, they served overcooked spaghetti. Fridays, we were lucky. We got treated to soggy pizza that stuck to the roof of your mouth. Free lunch in Detroit public schools was one step up from food they serve in jail. But compared to the potatoes I was eating at home, free lunch was usually the most nutritious meal of my day. The real problem was, I only got free lunch when school was in session. Between June and September, Mama was supposed to give me lunch money. But, somehow, she never seemed to remember. Instead, I had to fend for myself, which meant there were plenty of days I went hungry.

I try not to blame her. Taking care of two kids on a low-paying job all on your own has to be stressful. That's probably why, when it came to parenting duties, my mother opted for a hands-off approach. She put a roof over our heads and let Mrs. Brooks raise me when I was little. But as soon as I was old enough to reach the faucets on the bathtub and climb on a chair to stir a pot on the stove, my mother tapped out of most basic mothering duties. She didn't help me with my homework, make my bed, or do my laundry. Instead, I washed my own clothes with a washboard in the bathtub and hung them over the shower rod to dry. We never ate dinner together or watched TV as a family. Sometimes, it felt like she forgot I was alive.

I admit, there were times I felt sorry for myself. I wanted a different kind of mother, one more like Florida Evans from *Good Times* who looked like she'd do anything for her kids. But you don't get to choose your parents. You get what you get and you have to figure out the rest. Having a mama who forgot to keep me fed did have one upside, though. It's how I learned a valuable lesson: I would make a shitty-ass criminal.

I thought all the kids who got free lunch at Foster Elementary struggled the same way I did. But the summer between second and third grade I noticed that a lot of my friends seemed to be eating just fine. I'd see them at the corner store buying themselves all kinds of goodies: Better Made barbeque potato chips, Hostess cherry pies with real fruit filling, Vernor's ginger ale, and Chick-O-Sticks for dessert.

"Where'd you get money for all that?" I asked Peaches one day when I saw her in the store paying for a package of Drake's Devil Dogs and a can of Spam.

"Found it," she said.

"Found it where?" I asked.

"In my mama's purse."

A few days later, I saw Mavis and Marvell feasting on saltine crackers, Orange Crush, and a tin of Vienna sausages. "Where'd you get the cash to pay for all that?" I asked.

"Found it," Mavis said with a shrug.

"Where?"

"Uncle Freddy's pants pocket."

"The pocket on the left side," offered Marvell, "right where he keeps his bus pass." She reached into her own pocket and pulled out Uncle Freddy's pass. "You need a ride?"

The next week, Willy Williams showed up at the corner store waving a thick book of food stamps. "I'm rich!" he announced, fanning the stamps like a stack of singles at a strip club. "What you want, Loni?" he asked with a grin. "Get anything you like. I gotchu, girl!"

"Where'd you get all that?" I asked. Those stamps were enough to keep us fed with Honey Buns, Ho Hos, and Fanta for an entire month.

"In my granny's hiding place," Willy replied.

"Where's that?"

"In her bra, between her titties," he explained. "I waited till she fell asleep and then," he flicked his wrist and snapped his fingers, "bam! Took 'em. They mine now."

It turns out that while I was practically starving to death, all the other kids were running a petty theft hustle, swiping lunch money from their family members. In other neighborhoods, kids don't have to resort to a life of crime. They get handouts called "weekly allowance" given to them by their parents. That's middle-class welfare, if you ask me. In Brewster-Douglass, kids had to be resourceful if they wanted to get fed. Apparently, I was the only one who didn't know what was up.

"Check between your mama's titties," Willy advised. "Or look in her dresser next to where she keeps her drawers. Ladies always hide their money near their titties or their cooch; that's a fact. You better get you some," he added, handing me a bag of Cheez Balls and a can of 7Up. "How else you gonna eat?" Willy had a point. If Mama wasn't going to feed me, I was going to have to get money some kind of way. I had nothing to lose but my empty belly.

Early the next morning when I was sure my mother was in the shower, I tiptoed into her bedroom to check her underwear drawer for money, like Willy said. When I stepped inside her room, I couldn't believe my luck. Lying right there on top of her dresser, beside a thin leather wallet I'd never seen before, were two single dollar bills and a handful of loose coins. This was a sign from God, I decided. In His infinite wisdom, God had put the cash right there for me to take. I cocked my head, checking for the sound of the shower. Hearing running water and my mother giggling to herself behind the closed bathroom door, I quickly swiped three quarters, four dimes, and a nickel from her dresser and ran back into my room.

God is good, I thought to myself later that day, as I enjoyed the Little Debbie Swiss Roll and Dr. Pepper I'd bought myself for lunch, *and so is stealing.*

After that, executing in-home unarmed robbery became a regular thing for me. Anytime I saw some money lying out on Mama's dresser, I'd sneak in and pocket a few coins or the occasional dollar bill. I kept my hard-earned cash in my personal savings account: wedged under my bed, between my mattress and box spring. I was swiping enough money to finance corner-store lunch on the regular. But I was also saving up for something big.

About five blocks away from where we lived, down on Woodward Avenue, was a gleaming White Castle. I'd never been to that fine dining establishment before. But I'd seen the mouth-watering commercials on TV and I knew exactly what I wanted to order: four sliders, an order of fries, and an ice-cold Fanta. I would lie in bed at night dreaming about that lunch the way some kids dream about unicorns. And I might have lived to see my food fantasy come true if only I hadn't been caught.

To this day, I don't know who tipped off Mama, or if she figured it out herself. All I know is she came stomping into my room one morning at the crack of dawn so furious I could practically see the steam coming out of her ears. She knew exactly where to look, too. She lifted up my mattress and pointed an accusing finger at the evidence of my crime spree: two single dollar bills and thirty-eight cents in coins.

"You stealin'?" she demanded.

"No," I lied, my heart pounding hard in my chest. *This is it,* I thought. *I'm eight years old and I'm going into cardiac arrest.* I closed my eyes and prayed she would take pity on me and call for an ambulance.

"Then where did you get this money from?" Mama asked, with death rays shooting from her eyes.

"I . . . I . . . ," I stammered, clutching my ponytails in fear.

That's when I discovered that, unlike my thieving friends, I am not cut out for a life of crime. I don't have the nerves. If the authorities ever got me in one of those *Law & Order* interrogation situations, I'd be confessing to everything—robbery, embezzlement, arson, election rigging—just to get the cops to stop asking me questions. Standing in my bedroom with my mother glaring at me, I folded like a house of cards.

"I did it!" I blurted out, covering my face with my hands. "I took the money. I was hungry."

My mother was not moved. She grabbed me by the arm and marched me into her bedroom. To my surprise, sitting on the edge of her bed, tying up his shoes, was some guy I'd never seen before. "This is your uncle Joe," Mama said. "It's his money you took. Tell him you're sorry and give it back."

I shuffled over to Uncle Joe with my head hung low. "I'm sorry," I mumbled, handing over his change.

Joe leaned his head toward mine. "Let me give you a tip, little lady," he whispered into my ear in a deep, gravelly voice. "Next time you tryna' jack a nigga, you best find a better hiding place than under your mattress. That's the first place anybody's gonna look. Use your head."

"Thank you," I whispered. "I'll do better next time."

I turned to my mother, who was standing in the doorway with her arms folded across her chest. "I'm sorry, Mama," I said. "I'll never do it again."

Back in my room, I sat on my bed totally confused. My friends were telling me that if I wanted to eat, crime was the answer; my mother was telling me not to steal; this Joe dude was saying that the real problem was I was doing it all wrong. All I knew for sure is that if I wanted to eat, I was going to need a miracle.

God must have known I needed help because not too long after I got busted in-house for robbery, the good Lord sent one of his people my way to make sure I got fed.

The first time I heard Miss Eva ring her big brass school bell, I was standing at the edge of the Brewster-Douglass playground—aka the most dangerous place on earth.

I haven't spent a whole lot of time in playgrounds in the suburbs, but I imagine they have all kinds of fancy shit, like fresh mowed grass, velvet-lined monkey bars, and hired help to spot the kids as they go down the slide. By comparison, at the Brewster-Douglass playground—which was located in the middle of an asphalt courtyard that ran between the buildings—all we had was a rickety swing set and a rusty jungle gym covered in peeling paint. There was not a blade of grass in sight, and the entire place smelled like piss courtesy of JoJo the Wino, who used the playground as his personal toilet and crash pad for sleeping off his hangovers. In the mornings, we'd find him passed out under the slide. On the playground, drunk-ass JoJo was as close as we kids got to adult supervision.

You want to know why kids from Brewster-Douglass were so badass? It's not poverty and broken homes that hardened us; it's the fact that we were forced to risk our lives every time we tried to play. Willy Williams lost his two front teeth the day the crusty chain on the swing set finally snapped. My friend Peaches gave herself a concussion falling off the slide. And Miss French's daughter Mavis almost lost an eye when one of the swings snapped off its chain and hit her in the face. That place was a death trap.

I used to spend a lot of time standing on the sidelines of the playground, leaning against a metal pole where a chain-link fence used to be, trying to figure out my odds of playing on the jungle gym and making it out alive. Like, *If there are five kids on the monkey bars and so far only two have fallen off . . . wooooah, make that three . . . the odds are not in my favor today!* Calculating my risk of injury and dismemberment is exactly what I was doing the day I first heard Miss Eva's bell.

It was early July, and school had been out for weeks, but that bell sounded just like the one my teachers rang to call us in from recess. I looked around, trying to see where the sound was coming from. That's when I saw a little gray-haired lady I recognized from building 6 standing beside a picnic table under a wooden structure we called "the Shed" that offered the only shade in the courtyard. She had a shopping cart with her and was ringing her big brass school bell.

"Time for Bible study!" she called. "Come on up, children. It's time to study Scripture!"

This lady has lost her entire mind, I thought. You'd have to be crazy to think that a group of sweaty kids on summer break would stop playing just to sit with an old lady to read the—

"I got ice cream!" she called out. "Ice cream for anyone who joins me for Bible study. Come and get it, children. It sure is hot today!" Suddenly, half a dozen kids, including me, were running toward the Shed like they'd heard gunshots. I wasn't very athletic—unless you count the time I had to carry my French horn up seven flights of stairs when our building's elevators went out—but hearing the phrase "ice cream" sent me sprinting to that picnic table like Flo-Jo.

"Welcome, children, I'm Miss Eva," the lady said with a big smile. "I'm so happy you decided to join me on this glorious day. Praise be. Today we are going to study the Twenty-Third Psalm. It's one of my very favorites." Miss Eva reached into her shopping cart with her wrinkled hands and pulled out a stack of worn Bibles and passed them around. She explained that at the end of Bible study, we'd each get an ice cream cone. "I've got my cooler right here," she said, pointing to her buggy. "Now don't that sound good?"

People think the projects are filled with drug dealers and gang-bangers. But at Brewster-Douglass we had Gospel Gangsters, too. My babysitter Miss Brooks's hustle was to ambush people in their own homes and kill them with kindness until they agreed to read *The Watchtower*. Miss Eva specialized in straight-up bribery. She told us she was going to hold Bible study every Sunday morning for the rest of the summer. Not only would she give us ice cream cones just for showing up, she said, if any of us could recite a psalm from memory, she'd bless us with an extra scoop. I raised my hand. "Is this a onetime offer?" I asked. "Or will you be giving out extra scoops every Sunday?"

Miss Eva cocked her head to the side as though she were thinking it over. "Loni," she said, "I like your spirit! Yes, indeed. Those who put in the effort will always be rewarded. Any child able to recite a psalm from memory will get an extra scoop, today and every Sunday!"

I couldn't believe my luck. I shot up my hand again. "I can say the Twenty-Third Psalm by heart," I announced. I quickly stood up, clasped my hands together in prayer position, and began to recite: "The Lord is my Shepherd, I lack nothing. He makes me lie down in green pastures, he leads me beside quiet waters, he refreshes my soul..."

"That was wonderful," Miss Eva said when I was done. She gave me a double scoop of chocolate ice cream for my efforts. I killed it that first day of Bible study summer camp. And I kept killing it all summer long. No matter which passage Miss Eva wanted us to study, I already knew it, thanks to Mrs. Brooks.

Folks say God acts in mysterious ways and that eventually all will be revealed. The summer I turned nine, I had my first God-related revelation: All those afternoons I'd spent learning Scripture with Miss Brooks when I was little weren't only to save my soul. They were also because God wanted me to have nice things, like ice cream. That's when I became a true believer.

By the time school started that fall, I had gained ten pounds. I call it my Bible weight. I used to think God sent me Miss Eva and all that delicious ice cream to give me a head start on my Big Girl Life. But I know now He had a bigger message: when you're desperate, doing the wrong thing sometimes looks like the best solution, but have faith that God will show you another way.

Hard-Knock Life

There's a lot of stuff you learn growing up in the projects that you wish you didn't know:

- What government cheese tastes like
- Where to buy a loosie
- Which crackheads have the lowest prices on gently used appliances
- The time of day the elevator in your building has the least amount of piss
- How to do your homework when the electricity gets turned off
- That an open fire hydrant is the neighborhood spa
- That ketchup can be used as a condiment, sandwich filling, main entrée, and household epoxy
- When the TV set breaks down, it instantly becomes a TV stand for the new set

CHAPTER 4

FIND YOUR HUSTLE

Not everyone at Brewster-Douglass was poor. Sometimes we had visitors. Like Amber Davis, the classiest ten-year-old I've ever known.

I met Amber at Miss Eva's Bible-study–Scripture-reading summer youth outreach bribery camp. She lived with her mother, a receptionist at a law firm, in a fancy apartment building downtown. Every morning during summer break, Ms. Davis would bring Amber to stay with her grandmother, who lived in one of the low-rise apartments on the north side of the projects. The first time I saw Amber, I knew she was different. She had the put-together look of Lauryn and Charlotte from Girl Scouts camp. But she was even *more* fly. The day we met, Amber was wearing beige corduroy culottes with electric-green knee socks that matched her plastic barrettes. Another day she wore a red polka-dotted skirt and vest set with matching red Mary Janes. I didn't know any kids who dressed in shoes that matched their outfits unless they were going someplace special, like school graduation or to testify in family court. But Amber had style for days. She looked like what would happen if Dee from *What's Happening!* got dressed by Diana Ross.

The other kids at Bible study took one look at Amber and decided to ignore her. She looked different and nobody had time for her uppity ass. But I wanted to give Amber a chance. I appreciated the way she listened respectfully during Miss Eva's teachings. And I especially liked the way she leaned over in my direction and whispered, "Good job!" whenever I finished reciting a Bible passage by heart. I'd never heard anybody but teachers say, "Good job." Amber talked like she was grown.

The two of us grew close that summer. When we weren't in Bible study, we'd play jacks or jump rope or flip through Amber's copies of *Right On!* magazine and argue about which Jackson brother was the cutest. Amber liked Michael.

"He looks so nice," she'd say dreamily, tracing his picture on the page. "Don't his Afro look just like a halo? It's like he flew down from heaven." I thought Michael was all right. But I favored Tito. I liked the way he lay in the cut with his guitar. As a musician who appreciated an instrument that you can rest on your lap, I respected Tito's low-key vibe.

When school started up again in the fall, Amber and I stayed friends. I'd see her on the weekends, when she came to visit her grandmother. One time she invited me over to her place to hang out after school. Amber's was the first apartment I'd ever set foot in that wasn't in the projects. The building had a doorman dressed in a green jacket and cap. Before I was allowed on the elevator, he called up to announce my arrival: "I have a Miss Loni here to see you." It felt like I was visiting George and Weezy Jefferson's deluxe apartment in the sky. I almost expected their maid, Florence, to greet me at the door.

Before I'd been to Amber's place, the only thing I knew about black life outside the projects is what I learned watching *The Jeffersons* and *Diff'rent Strokes*. But neither of those shows prepared me for the up-close-and-personal luxury of Amber's mama's apartment. Ms. Davis, who liked to rock a platinum-blond Marilyn Monroe wig, had decorated her living room in creamy shades of white. There was a shiny white lacquered coffee table, an extra-cushy off-white leather sofa, and cream-colored carpeting, fluffier than anything I'd ever stepped on. It felt like everywhere I looked were magical items of home decor: red velvet throw pillows, miniature glass figurines, a wood-paneled hi-fi stereo console, and heavy drapes hanging in the windows. At my place, all the furniture came from the Goodwill and was covered in plastic. Our brown rug was thin and decorated in beer stains from Mama's Friday night get-togethers. Instead of drapes, we had crooked venetian blinds. No matter how hard I tugged at the strings, those blinds stayed slanted, like a triple-beam scale.

Sometimes I'd get a stomachache when I visited Amber. But it wasn't from all the chocolate milk and Pringles her mama let us eat. My bellyaches were pangs of jealousy I'd get seeing all the things Amber had that I wished I had myself. Amber had her own bedroom with a canopy bed; a desk where she could do her homework that was fully stocked with all kinds of school supplies, including a matching stapler and pencil sharpener set; and a toybox full of board games and Barbie dolls. But what I coveted most was what lay behind the double doors of her bedroom closet. Amber had a wardrobe more beautiful than anything I could ever have imagined, filled with neon-colored skirt and sweater sets and candy-colored jeans. She had pink jellies, blue Keds, and red knee-high cowboy boots. She even had clothes hanging in her closet with the price tags still attached. I had never seen anything like it. I wanted some fancy-ass clothes more than anything. By the time I started high school I was so damn tired of dressing like I was poor.

Amber and I didn't go to the same elementary school or junior high. But when I was fourteen, I scored high enough on a city test to get into Cass Technical magnet school, one of the best public high schools in Detroit. Amber went there, too. In fact, the entire school was filled with Ambers—middle-class kids with laid hair and matching outfits. You know all those John Hughes movies where the high school is divided into jocks, nerds, goths, and stoners? Cass Technical was like that, too. Except we were all black.

There was a clique of kids who thought they were "down" and dressed like members of Electric Boogaloo, in bright pink parachute pants and bandanas around their El DeBarge perms. We also had the Jack-and-Jill preppy contingent, looking like Carlton and Hilary Banks from the *Fresh Prince of Bel-Air.* And we had nerds like me, kids who played in the school's orchestra, or joined the math club, and looked like they didn't care how they dressed. Only I *did* care.

My dream was to go to school rocking a pair of Gloria Vanderbilt jeans. Those jeans, with the little embroidered swan on the front pocket and crisp white stitching that ran up the leg, were *everything*. In the TV commercials, Gloria and all her leggy model friends looked beautiful and smiled like they didn't have a care in the world. I thought if I wore those jeans,

I'd be happy, too. The problem was, those designer jeans cost thirty-four dollars. I knew if I asked Mama to buy me a pair, she'd just laugh in my face. Thirty-four dollars was her entire budget for my school clothes for the whole year—including shoes and a winter coat. We did all our shopping at Lucille's secondhand store, the kind of place folks nowadays might call a "vintage shoppe." But back then, secondhand was not a good look. Everything I owned was a decade out of fashion. In 1986, when girls at school were wearing leg warmers and ripped sweatshirts like they just walked off the set of *Flashdance,* I was rocking plaid bell bottoms and a wide-collared shirt. It's one thing to be the biggest girl in the class. It's another thing to be a big girl with a French horn dressed like a reject from season one of *Soul Train.*

I was convinced that the only way I was going to fit in, be happy, and have a good school life was if I could get me some of those GV jeans. All I had to do was figure out a way to make some cold, hard cash.

I was convinced that the only way I was going to fit in, be happy, and have a good school life was if I could get me some of those GV jeans. All I had to do was figure out a way to make some cold, hard cash.

Like a lot of places filled with poor folks, Brewster-Douglass had its own underground economy. There was the Candy Lady, who would buy Blow Pops, Now and Laters, and Double Bubble in bulk and then sell them to children for a nickel apiece; and ladies like Mrs. Brooks who took care of other people's kids. There was the Numbers Man, who ran the project's lottery system and off-track betting, and the guy with a toolbox, who did car repairs under a shade tree out by building number 6. The resident barber was some dude who set out a lawn chair in the courtyard, ran an extension cord through his front window, plugged in his clippers, and started charging for shape-ups. And on just about every floor of every building was an amateur beautician who did hair in her kitchen or painted nails in her living room. I even heard rumors of a lady who performed DIY abortions.

Of course, we had our share of drug dealers, too. As far as I could tell, they made their money mostly by selling weed. At least that's how things were until crack came to town.

Before crack happened, I didn't think too much about drugs or drinking. It was around, but it just wasn't a big deal. On Friday nights, Mama would put Earth Wind & Fire on her little record player and invite her friends over for "cocktail hour," which went until two in the morning. From the bedroom I shared with Bruce, I could hear the conversations grow louder and the laughter more rambunctious as the night wore on. The smell of weed would waft in like a skunk had sprayed the living room. Mama partied, but she and her friends never got out of hand. The worst thing that might happen is that Mama would be hungover and kind of wobbly on Saturday mornings when she was heating up the hot comb to press my hair. That's why to this day I wear my wigs long. I have Mama's-got-a-hangover burns all over the tops of my ears.

I'm not mad at her, though. Life in Brewster-Douglass wasn't easy. A little partying helped take the edge off. As far as I could tell, having a glass of E&J brandy and smoking a little weed didn't seem to hurt anybody. But in the mid-1980s, right around the time I started high school, crack landed in the neighborhood like a tornado, blowing everything apart. Crack isn't like weed or brandy; it's not for good times and get-togethers. Crack took people out.

In the beginning, I didn't notice what was going on. That's because some addicts were high-functioning, at least at first. Like Miss Ella, a school crossing guard who lived across the hall. She would get up, get dressed, do a hit, then head out to work. I didn't know she was using until I saw her cop a hit from a corner boy outside our building. In the early days of crack, there were all kinds of functioning addicts. They had jobs at local hospitals and day care centers or working on the General Motors assembly line. But those people were the exceptions. Most folks who messed with crack eventually got burned.

I'd see them out on the sidewalk—formerly normal-looking neighbors—all twitchy and stanky, with dirty clothes and matted hair. Or they'd be out on the corner in the middle of the day wandering around with a toaster, trying to sell it so they could buy themselves a five-dollar hit. The women were the saddest cases. Once they sold their church shoes, children's clothes, and small kitchen appliances, they'd be out in the middle of the day trying to sell themselves.

Crack didn't just destroy individual people. It impacted our entire community. People started robbing their own neighbors; teenage boys–turned–dealers started shooting in the streets; addict parents stopped taking care of their kids. More than a few times, I'd come home from school to see some toddler or infant getting taken away by a lady in a cheap blue pants suit who worked with Child Protective Services. The CPS lady spent so much time at Brewster-Douglass that she and JoJo the Wino were on a first name basis. "Good morning, Mr. JoJo," she'd say as she walked through the courtyard.

"Right back at you," he'd reply, "you baby-snatching ho."

For the longest time, I didn't understand why anyone would pick up a drug that would make them lose everything. Then one day after school, our next-door neighbor Miss Thomas stepped into the elevator while I was riding up to my apartment. I hadn't seen her around in a while. I gave her a nod and a quick hello. "Loni," she said, looking at me with watery eyes. "Sometimes life hurts so bad you just want to escape."

"Yes, ma'am," I replied, not sure what she was talking about.

"It's just so hard," she continued, reaching out and putting a shaky hand to her lips. "I just want to forget." Only then did I notice how thin she'd become. Her skin was marked with sores and her fingers blackened from pipe burns. She wasn't even wearing her wig. Not long after that conversation, CPS took away Miss Thomas's children, too.

Looking back, I understand why Detroit got hit so hard by the crack epidemic. Crack is a drug of desperation. And back then, a lot of people were struggling more than they ever had before. The automotive industry, which for decades had been the city's major employer, with more than twenty plants in and around Detroit, was cutting back, and everywhere people were losing jobs. Detroit was in a financial free fall and folks at the bottom of the economic ladder had nothing to hold on to. Folks felt desperate, and like Miss Thomas said, crack helped them forget.

The city became a drug dealers' paradise. The Chambers brothers, who reportedly ran the largest crack distribution operation in American history, ran some of their multimillion-dollar enterprise out of properties they owned on the east side, not too far from Brewster-Douglass. One of the brothers, Billy Joe, ran a storefront on St. Clair and Kerchival that he named "B.J.'s Party Store," where he would package and sell his product. Most of it flowed right back into the projects. The crack economy made a lot of dealers rich.

At Brewster-Douglass, big-time dealers could find themselves clients and a workforce all at the same place. They'd get neighborhood kids to work for them as corner boys, lookouts, or drug runners, then turn around and sell crack to the parents of these very same kids. It was a vicious cycle, with the most ruthless dealers running the show. Sometimes, to recruit dope boys, dealers would entice them into the game by giving them a taste of how good their life could be. They'd buy kids new sneakers and clothes and let them drive their fancy cars. Once you've been ketchup-sandwich-poor, the promise of easy money is hard to resist.

One day after school, I was walking down Alfred Street carrying my French horn when I heard someone call my name. It was Willy Williams hollering to me from a shiny late-model Mercedes-Benz painted candy-apple red.

"Hey, girl!" he called as he inched his way down the street. "How you like me now?" Willy wasn't riding in the passenger seat, either. The dimple-faced boy I'd been crushing on since second grade was behind the wheel. Somebody with deep pockets had given fourteen-year-old Willy Williams keys to a brand-new car.

With all that drug money flowing like water, there was plenty of spillover for the girls. Girls like my friend Peaches, who were pretty, or fast, could get themselves a drug-dealing boyfriend. If you were a girl like me—rocking secondhand clothes, wearing glasses, and carrying around a big-ass French horn—the best you could hope for was a position as the BFF of a girl who had a drug-dealing boyfriend. That way you could at least hear about what it was like to have money to burn.

One night, Peaches came by my place licking her fingers and smacking her lips. Her dealer boyfriend had taken her to Joe Muer, a fancy seafood restaurant I could only dream about.

"They got this butter sauce," she explained, reciting the entire menu. "It's for dipping your food. That's how they do it in France. Come with me next time," she added. "Girl, I know you want to."

Peaches wasn't wrong. Crab legs in melted butter sure sounded better than the potato soup Mama had simmering on the stove. Hanging out with Peaches and her drug-dealer boyfriend was a tempting offer. And I might have taken Peaches up on it if not for Miss Thomas. After seeing her sadness in the elevator that day, I knew I didn't want any part of the crack economy.

Peaches thought I was crazy. She'd come by and show me all the clothes and shoes and makeup her man had bought her and invite me shopping, too. But as much as I wanted to get me some Gloria Vanderbilts, I just couldn't do it. I had to find a hustle of my own.

⟋

I came up with the idea for my one-woman business enterprise almost by accident. It was a rainy Sunday afternoon and Mama asked me to help out our elderly neighbor Miss Hill by picking up a few groceries for her at the corner store. Miss Hill gave me her list—Vienna sausages, dried spaghetti, white bread, two bananas, and a can of Spam—and enough food stamps to cover the cost. When I delivered the groceries to her door, she thanked me and pressed a dollar bill into my hand, my tip for a job well done.

That's when I got the idea. If I could deliver five bags of groceries a week, at a dollar a pop, I could make enough money to buy myself those GV jeans in less than two months. I spun around and knocked on Miss Hill's door. "Would you tell your friends I'm available for shopping any day of the week?" I said. "I can pick up all their groceries." I scrawled my house phone number on a piece of paper and told her to pass it on.

Business started out slow. At first, I got only a couple of calls a week. (This was before you could depend on fake Yelp reviews to build a brand. Back then, all I had was word of mouth.) But I was determined to make that money, so I did what any entrepreneur would do: I started to advertise. Tearing pages from my spiral notebook, I made dozens of flyers for "Loni's Delivery Service: For All Your Shopping Needs" and passed them out after school. Soon enough, all kinds of senior citizens were blowing up Mama's phone.

I noticed that business picked up whenever the weather was bad, so I began to do "targeted marketing." In my best penmanship, I handwrote a bunch of new flyers: "That can of Spam is not worth a slip and fall!" I was probably the only kid in the projects who prayed for rain.

By January, winter weather was in full effect and I was making close to twenty dollars a week. Pushing my little shopping cart with a stack of one-dollar bills in my pocket, I felt like a mogul. Maybe I was walking with a little too much confidence because one afternoon, Peaches's boyfriend D'Vonte pulled up beside me. He was driving a midnight-blue BMW with tinted windows and custom rims.

"Hey, girl," he said, leaning his head out the driver's-side window. "I hear you run a delivery service."

I had never in my life talked to D'Vonte before. I'd seen him with Peaches, but he'd never so much as looked in my direction. "Yeah," I answered, gesturing at my shopping cart. "I run this."

"So, what you make a week?"

I shrugged. I wasn't about to reveal my financials to D'Vonte and let him in on the inner workings of my delivery empire. After all, I had cornered the market. My business was popping. I wondered if maybe he was asking because he wanted a piece of my action? Of course, there was no way I was going to partner up with a drug dealer. But I might let him *buy* my delivery service for the right price. I'd have to tell him about my customers' preferences and special requests, like how Miss Moore refused to buy her groceries from the store on the corner because she said the clerk was "slick." Instead, she made me walk an extra half mile, all the way to a store near Eastern Market, to get her wheat bread and skim milk. Or how Miss Brandell only ever wanted me to pick up cigarettes and cat food even though she didn't own a cat.

D'Vonte leaned his head farther out the window and looked up and down the block, as if he was scanning for cops. That's when I noticed Willy Williams riding shotgun. Willy looked good, with the same wide smile and dimples that made me fall for him in second grade. He gave me a nod and I waved back. "So, listen up," D'Vonte said to me. "How'd you like to make some *real* coin?"

Oh my God, is this really happening? I thought. Did D'Vonte want to buy my business? If I could do this deal, I could buy an entire wardrobe, instead of saving up for a month for a single pair of jeans.

"I could set you up real nice," he continued. "You wouldn't even have to push that piece-of-shit cart."

I didn't appreciate D'Vonte criticizing my shopping cart. But I kept my focus on the negotiation. "How much are you willing to pay?" I asked. "I have a lot of customers. So, I'm not trying to sell my business for cheap. It's gonna cost you."

D'Vonte stared at me, confused. "Wait...," he said, a slow grin creeping across his face. "You think I want to deliver *food*?" He threw back his head and howled so hard he could barely catch his breath. "Girl, have you lost your damn mind?"

This time it was my turn to be confused. "You asked me if I wanted to make some money," I said. "I thought you wanted to buy my business. What are *you* talking about?"

"I was talking about you working for *me*," he said. "You might run that little shopping cart but I run this whole block."

Suddenly, Willy leaned over, shaking his head. "Nah, man," he said to D'Vonte. "You do not want Loni working for you." He hesitated, as if searching for the right word. "She's a *nerd*, man. Like, straight up. You don't want her."

Standing on the street corner with Willy insulting me and D'Vonte laughing his ass off, I felt my face grow hot. I was used to guys like D'Vonte making fun of me. You don't lug a French horn through the projects without growing a thick skin. Boys had been teasing me for years, calling out "Nerd alert!" whenever I walked by. But I thought Willy and I were cool.

"Don't bother with her," he said to D'Vonte. "She ain't worth the trouble." D'Vonte looked me up and down and let out another snort. Then he hit the gas and took off.

It would be a few years before I realized that Willy was actually doing me a favor. He knew the temptation of easy drug money—hell, working for D'Vonte would have had me living that butter-sauce life instead of hustling for tips from senior citizens. But Willy also knew the risks. D'Vonte was mixed up in all kinds of dirty deals.

One night a few weeks later, I was lying in bed, when I heard the blasts of semiautomatic gunfire. It wasn't unusual to hear shots at Brewster-Douglass. But that night the sound filled me with dread.

The next morning, I learned that D'Vonte had been involved in a drive-by. A gang of rival dealers had rolled up on him as he sat in the courtyard, spraying bullets everywhere. One of the bullets meant for D'Vonte had hit my friend Peaches, instead. She was sixteen years old.

Child Labor

Forget paper routes and lemonade stands; in the projects, kids had to get creative if they wanted to earn a few bucks. Here are Brewster-Douglass kids' first-time jobs:

- Massaging old people's bunions
- Selling your free lunch to a fat kid at school
- Going to a fountain in the nice part of town and stealing people's wishes
- Volunteering as a dependent child for the tax write-off
- Selling your clean pee to folks who got drug-tested at work

CHAPTER 5

IN AND OUT OF MAMA'S HOUSE

Miss Davis used to call me and Amber "two peas in a pod." That's because I spent most of high school hanging out at Amber's place, luxuriating on her mama's soft-as-hell living room rug, drinking chocolate milk, and leafing through issues of *Right On!* magazine. Miss Davis didn't seem to mind at all. In fact, she treated me almost like I was family. She's the one who got me a cake on my fifteenth birthday, and when she left cash on the kitchen counter for Amber to go to White Castle after school, she always left enough money for me to get something to eat, too.

Miss Davis also introduced me to all kinds of culture. She took me and Amber to see the movie *The Color Purple* and the musical *Dreamgirls* and bought us tickets to our first live concert, Rick James. Amber and I were so naïve, we thought when Rick sang about being "in love with Mary Jane" that he was talking about a girl. Imagine our surprise when he performed the song with two six-foot-tall joints blowing fake smoke all over the stage.

I loved Miss Davis for her generosity. But what impressed

me even more was the way she treated her child. I noticed the little things—like the way she stuck Amber's good grades on the front of her refrigerator and told her daughter she looked "stunning" even when she just looked okay. Miss Davis always had a smile and kind word for Amber. By comparison, by the time I was in high school, my relationship with my mother had sunk to an all-time low.

My brother Bruce had moved out years before, so it was just me and Mama living in that tiny apartment like two roommates who have nothing in common. Sometimes, we'd cross paths on the way to the bathroom in the morning. "Hi, Mama," I'd say.

"Pick your clothes off the floor," she'd answer back. "Your room is a damn mess." And that would be our mother-daughter bonding for the week. Mama didn't even seem to get any pleasure out of things that mothers are *supposed* to enjoy—like helping her only daughter pick out a dress for senior prom.

Based on my extensive TV viewing, I knew prom dress shopping was supposed to be me in a dressing room trying on one prom dress after another while my mother waited to see how beautiful I looked, with her hands clasped together in eager anticipation. But it turns out my mother did not give even the tiniest of shits about what dress I wore to senior prom. She didn't work her ass off doing double shifts at the hospital just so she could spend her good and hard-earned money on a prom dress I would only wear once. Instead, I had to make my dress myself.

Hunched over a sewing machine in Home Economics class, I pieced together a gown of my own design. The dress was light purple satin with cap sleeves and a sweetheart neckline. Thanks to Mrs. Brooks's constant preaching on the importance of respectable attire, I made sure the top half of my dress revealed no more than a hint of cleavage. The business half of my gown was built like Fort Knox, with enough layers of wire hoops, crinoline, and lace to create an impenetrable barricade between my private treasure trove and any boy who might get the notion to grind up on me. I finished off my outfit with a pair of pristine white gloves. While the other girls at prom looked like they'd just finished their shift at LeRoy's Gentlemen's Club, I looked like I'd wandered off the set of *Gone with the Wind*.

This is the kind of fashion disaster a parent is supposed to protect her child from making. But Mama didn't care. By the time I was a senior in high school, she'd found Tyrone. Once he started coming around, I might as well have been invisible.

⌒

Tyrone was the first steady boyfriend in Mama's life since Uncle Chico walked out on her almost a decade before. She never sat me down and told me she had a new man. I simply came home from school one day and found Tyrone sitting on the sofa marking up a thick textbook with a green highlighter.

"Don't make no noise," Mama said, putting her finger to her lips. "Tyrone is studying."

"Who the hell is Tyrone?" I asked.

My mother ignored the question. Instead, she told me proudly, "Tyrone's taking his test to be a deputy sheriff." She said it with such satisfaction, as though she'd really accomplished something with her life by having a wannabe sheriff's second-hand man studying on her sofa. I rolled my eyes and went to my room. The next day when I came home from school,

Tyrone was there again, planted on the sofa with his textbook in his lap. He was there again the day after that. Eventually, I figured out that Tyrone wasn't just Mama's boyfriend; the dude had moved in.

I had nothing against Tyrone. He was never mean or nasty to me. But it's not like we bonded, either. I'd come home and he'd barely acknowledge me other than to glance up from his book. As far as I was concerned, he was just there, like another piece of furniture. I did wonder about his study habits, though. One time, I caught a glimpse of the book he was reading. He had highlighted the entire page, from top to bottom, in green marker. Every word.

"Aren't you supposed to highlight only the important stuff?" I asked.

"Yeah, well this all looks important to me," he snapped, continuing to color. I couldn't help but notice the annoyed look he shot my mother, like *I* was the one with the problem. He did that a lot.

Tyrone was a highlighting fool, but Mama loved him, none-theless. Or, at least, she loved that she finally had a man. At Brewster-Douglass, you could find plenty of young boys and senior-citizen men. But healthy adult males, like Tyrone, were in short supply. Growing up, I didn't know any kids who had their daddies in the house. And I didn't know any women my mother's age who had husbands, or even steady boyfriends. Men would come and go. Sometimes they got lost to drugs or violence. But mostly, they got locked up.

In Detroit, the cops had a long history of bad relations with black folks. In fact, a few years before I was born, in 1967, police brutality against black residents led to one of the largest uprisings in modern US history. Over five days of protests, local police and armed forces killed thirty residents, almost all of them black. Race relations in the city—which were already bad—never recovered. Cops would arrest black men for every damn thing. Just because they could. During the 1980s, black men in Michigan State were incarcerated at five times the rate of white men. There's only one way to explain that kind of discrepancy.

In Brewster-Douglass, we all knew the reason there were so few men around was that for years cops had been on a mission to throw their black asses in jail. So, it only made sense that Mama felt like she'd hit the jackpot with Tyrone. He wasn't locked up. He had all his teeth. And, sure, maybe he didn't have a job, but he was *thinking* about getting a job. He was employed adjacent.

Mama treated Tyrone like a king. One day, I opened the fridge looking for something to eat. I was shocked to find a plate piled high with baked chicken, greens, and mac and cheese. It looked like Christmas dinner in July. "Don't touch that!" Mama yelled, from the living room. "It's not for you. I cooked that for Tyrone."

Mama bought Tyrone a Trapper Keeper binder and a stack of index cards to help him study for his test. She rubbed the back of his neck when he was tired and served him home-cooked meals that included all the food groups, not just potatoes. I had never seen Mama so loving and attentive. She sure as hell didn't pay that kind of attention to me.

When you're a kid, you learn a lot about love and relationships by watching the adults around you. When something's wrong, you might not be able to put it into words, but you feel it in your body. I knew the way my mother was putting Tyrone above me was wrong. I knew the way she dropped everything to make sure he was okay while ignoring all my prom dress needs was not the way a good mama takes care of her child. But what could I do? You can't tell a mother to love her kids harder, and you can't tell a woman to love her man less. If you're raised by a parent who doesn't show you the love you deserve, you have to put your head down and remind yourself every day that their weakness is not a reflection on your worth.

Of course, I didn't know that at seventeen. All I knew was that Mama put a roof over my head. And if that was all she was offering, I sure as hell was gonna take it.

More than anything, I didn't want what happened to my brother Bruce to happen to me.

Bruce hadn't lived with us since he was eighteen, but he didn't move out of his own accord. Mama kicked him out because he didn't have a job. She said she wasn't trying to have a "grown man eating her out of house and home." Lucky for Bruce, Mrs. Brooks was able to find him a place to stay with a Jehovah's Witness family. But I wasn't trying to get put out like Bruce.

The day after I graduated, I opened up the *Detroit Free Press* and started scanning the help-wanted ads to find myself a job. I saw ads for minimum-wage positions, like fry cook at a fast-food restaurant or overnight janitor at a nursing home. Then, lower down on the page, was a listing for a job working the assembly line at the General Motors Detroit-Hamtramck plant, one of the last automotive factories to open in Detroit. My heart stopped when my eyes landed on the most beautiful words I'd ever seen in print: "Starting pay: $18 an hour, plus overtime."

Assembly-line worker wasn't a job I'd dreamed about when I was growing up. But this was the 1980s, the country was in a recession, and good-paying jobs were hard to come by, especially in Detroit. By the time I graduated Cass Tech, the once-thriving auto industry was barely hanging on. The brand-new plant in Detroit-Hamtramck had been built only after a special deal with the government allowed GM to take over a plot of land that used to be a neighborhood called Poletown. GM demolished 1,500 homes, 144 businesses, and sixteen churches and forced thousands of residents to relocate. It was all over the news. Detroit politicians hailed the Hamtramck plant as a last-ditch effort to revive the economy. But working at GM was no picnic. Next to cleaning up the rec center as a Girl Scout, busting my ass on that assembly line was the hardest labor I've ever done.

The GM plant, which produced boxy Cadillac Eldorados, operated like its own little city, with more than a thousand workers doing shifts around the clock. This was before automation took hold, so every car that left the factory was put together by hand. Workers in one part of the factory were responsible for getting the cars painted; other workers were in charge of assembling the chassis. I worked in the trim department, which is where we focused on the car interiors—everything from installing the seats to screwing in the rearview mirrors. For twelve hours a day, six days a week, I hot-glued five hundred pieces of carpeting onto five hundred Cadillac doors.

The work was tedious and tiring as hell, but it wasn't rocket science. Once I got the hang of the glue gun, there really wasn't much else I needed to learn. There were plenty of days when my biggest challenge was simply getting to work on time.

To make it to my six a.m. shift, I had to wake up at four thirty, walk twenty-five minutes across a footbridge that ran over four lanes of the Walter P. Chrysler Freeway to Eastern Market, make my way to the corner of Mack Avenue and John R. Street, where I would catch the city bus and then ride it sixteen stops to Grand Street, then walk another fifteen minutes to the plant.

By bus, it took almost an hour for me to get to work, longer if there was snow on the ground. By car, the trip was only fifteen minutes. But there wasn't a cab service in town that would pick up passengers in the projects. During one really bad snowstorm, I offered Tyrone twenty-five dollars to drive me to work, but Mama said no, Tyrone needs his rest. I guess highlighting his damn textbook took all his energy.

I hated Tyrone for not driving me to work. But in the end, it turns out he was doing me a favor. If it wasn't for his "resting," I might never have bought myself a car.

During lunch break one day at the plant, Ray-Ray, who worked not far from me on the line, announced he was selling his ride. "It's a good deal," he said. "It's only got two hundred thousand miles on it!"

That 1979 Chevy Chevette piece-of-shit hoopty was the ugliest thing I'd ever seen. It was painted light blue except for the rear passenger door, which was inexplicably painted maroon. The floorboards were rusted out, the radio was busted, and there was a giant dent in the driver's-side door. Ray-Ray's ride looked like the kind of vehicle you'd see on the side of the highway, surrounded by cops and yellow tape.

"I'll take it," I said. It cost me all my savings—almost one thousand dollars—which I paid in cash. I thought anything was better than walking to the bus stop, in the cold, before the crack of dawn. But I didn't know then how bad things were about to get.

On a bitterly cold night in February, I'd just finished working a twelve-hour shift and was dead tired. As I pulled into the parking lot behind our building at Brewster-Douglass, all I could think about was peeling off my sweaty clothes, dropping them on the floor, and slipping into bed. My mother, however, had other ideas.

"LONI!!!" I heard her yell as I walked through the courtyard toward our building. She was calling from our living room window seven flights up, which means she'd been watching and waiting for me. "Get up here *now*!"

I waved to let her know I'd heard her as I made my way to our building's front door. I didn't know what Mama was hollering about, but I knew it couldn't be anything good. I wondered if I'd accidentally eaten some food she'd put aside for Tyrone. Or maybe I was brushing my teeth too loudly in the morning and disturbing his precious sleep. I stepped onto the elevator and felt the floor rumble as it climbed to the seventh floor. I was so exhausted, the last thing I needed was to get into a stupid argument. All I wanted was to take my ass to bed and get some sleep.

When the elevator doors slid open, I stepped off, walked slowly down the hallway, and turned the corner to our apartment. That's when I saw the row of overstuffed trash bags propped against the wall. There were half a dozen bags, at least. Lying haphazardly atop one of the black bags—as though it had been carelessly tossed on the pile—was a single white knock-off Keds women's sneaker, size 10. I recognized it immediately. I'd been looking for that missing tennis shoe for weeks! I stuck it under my arm as I pulled open the trash bag. Inside was a jumble of mismatched socks, T-shirts, bras, and shorts. I opened another bag and found an old winter jacket, a pair of child-sized hard-soled patent leather church shoes, and a crumpled eight-by-ten picture of Tito Jackson that I'd torn from one of Amber's *Right On!* magazines. In a third bag I discovered an algebra textbook, a pair of blue Cass Tech gym shorts, and my good Gloria Vanderbilt jeans. I felt myself getting hot with anger. Everything I owned in the entire world was in those bags. My mother had packed up my belongings and hadn't even bothered to fold anything. She just threw away my possessions like she was tossing out the trash, and I didn't know why.

I took a breath and pushed open the apartment door. Mama was standing in the middle of the living room with her hands on her hips. "You need to get your stuff and get on up out of here," she said.

"But *why*?" I asked. "I didn't do nothing!"

"It's my house," she said. "You need to go."

I knew plenty of girls who got put out of their mamas' houses. But there was always a reason. Juleen, who lived two floors up, got kicked out when her mother found out Juleen was pregnant. Sandra, who used to go to Miss Eva's Bible study summer camp with me and Amber, got kicked out when Sandra's mama found out *she* was pregnant. ("I've got a four-kid maximum," her mother said. "I gotta cut you loose.")

But I was a good girl. I didn't drink or do drugs or mess with boys. Thanks to my anti-fornication prom dress—and the fear of God Mrs. Brooks had put in me—I was still a virgin. Not only that, I had a job, I paid for my own food, and I stayed out of Mama's way. There was no reason on God's green earth that my mother should kick me out.

"I'm sick and tired of you leaving your clothes all over the floor," Mama continued. "You need to leave."

"You're kicking me out for not cleaning my room?" I asked, incredulous. This didn't make any sense.

Mama folded her arms in front of her chest. "This is *my* place," is all she had to say.

I stared at her in disbelief. From the corner of my eye, I could see Tyrone, who was chilling on the sofa, peering out from behind his textbook. He caught me looking at him and quickly turned away. That's when it hit me: This wasn't about me or my leaving clothes on the floor. This was about Tyrone. Mama was getting rid of me so she and Tyrone could be alone.

❧

Before Tyrone came along, my mother hadn't ever talked to me about love and relationships. She didn't tell me what to look for in a man or how I should be treated as a woman. But that night, it was like she was teaching me everything she wanted me to know: If you've got a man, don't let anything get in your way, she seemed to be saying. If it means you need to fix him Christmas dinner on a Tuesday in July, do it. If it means you have to put your only daughter out of the house so your dumb-ass man can have you all to himself, then you do that, too.

When I was younger, I used to tell myself that my mother didn't show her love like Amber's mother did because she was more of a silent type. But standing in her living room with all my possessions in trash bags in the hall, I couldn't help but wonder if maybe my mama didn't love me at all. I felt my eyes stinging and my throat getting tight. But there was no way in hell I was going to let my mother or Tyrone see me cry.

"Whatever," I said, heading for the door. "I gotta go before some crackhead steals my stuff."

I don't think my relationship with my mother ever recovered from that night. As much as I've thought about it, I've never asked if she worried about sending me into the cold with no place to go. I haven't asked because I don't want to know the answer. There's nothing that will mess with your head more than finding out your own mama didn't care.

Of course, there isn't a person in this world who doesn't have some pain they carry from childhood. I know a lot of folks had it way worse than I did. But we all have to figure out a way to get past the pain. For me, it helped to look at the wisdom I gained from having my mama kick me out when I was barely grown. I learned that sometimes—no matter how hard you try to play by the rules and do the right thing—life just ain't fair. That's a truth some people take a lifetime to learn. Thanks to my mama, I got the memo before my eighteenth birthday.

When life deals you a shitty hand—or a not-so-great parent—you have two choices: You can holler and cry about how you've been done wrong. Or you can play the hand you're dealt and figure out a way to pull yourself together and move forward. Sometimes that means you've got to spend a few nights sleeping in your car.

You Know You're a Bad Parent When...

- Your friends don't know you have a kid.
- Your kids can dance better than they can read.
- No one will babysit no matter how much you pay.
- Your kids know how to make a vodka martini.
- You step outside the club to check on your kids in the car.
- You spend more on your car than on your child.
- You call your child "D'Marws," but his name is "Frank."
- You can't remember who the daddy is.

CHAPTER 6

IF GOD SENDS YOU A SIGN, YOU BETTER PAY ATTENTION

"She dead?" I heard someone ask. I was barely awake, but I recognized the voice immediately. It was Angela, a friendly middle-aged woman who worked next to me on the assembly line at GM. Angela's job was to insert ashtrays and attach handles to the inside of the passenger-side doors; I installed window cranks and glued down little pieces of carpeting that ran along the bottom to finish off the trim.

"Nah," another voice replied. "She's breathing. Her chest is moving up and down. She got them big ole titties. Just look!"

For weeks, ever since my mother had kicked me out, I'd been sleeping in the employee parking lot at GM, or, as I liked to tell myself, taking "extended naps."

Every night after my shift, I would settle down in the front seat of my beat-up Chevy Chevette, close my eyes, and pray to God that I didn't get murdered in my sleep. It wasn't the best place for a teenage girl to call home, but I didn't have anywhere else to go.

After my mother told me to leave, I drove to a pay phone on the corner of Woodward Avenue and Michigan Street and called my aunt Ella to ask if I could stay with her. "No, girl," she'd said. "Your mama just called me. If you think I'm letting you come over here and make a mess of *my* place, you've got another thing coming."

Then I tried Amber's house, but no one picked up. For hours, I drove around the city not knowing where to go. I passed Foster Elementary on St. Antoine Street, the rec center on Chrysler Freeway Drive, and the boarded-up houses on Wilkins Street before it finally dawned on me that spending the night in the GM parking lot actually made good sense. Plenty of people napped in their cars during breaks, so I figured no one would think anything of it if they saw me asleep. Plus, there was a shower in the locker room where I could wash up before my shift. It turns out if your mama's gonna put you out of the house, it helps to have a full-time factory job.

I planned to spend only one night in the employee parking lot. But that night became two, which quickly stretched into four. Before I knew it, a month had passed by. I hated living out of my car. The only thing worse, I discovered when Angela started rapping loudly on my driver's-side window that day, was waking up to a crowd of people watching you sleep.

"Loni!" Angela yelled again. "Girl, wake the fuck up."

"I'm up!" I said, wiping the drool from the side of my mouth. I smoothed my hair, which was sticking up every which way—because that's what happens when you sleep with your face in the steering wheel—and pulled my seat into an upright position. "I was napping."

"Oh yeah?" Angela peered into the backseat, which was piled high with my belongings. "You always nap with all your clothes?"

"No . . . ," I said. "That's my laundry."

Angela crossed her arms in front of her chest. "That do not look like laundry to me," she said, with a snort. "You got books and shoes and shit all over the place. You got a toothbrush in your cup holder and a toaster on the dashboard." Angela shook her head. "Girlfriend, how you live is none of my business," she added. "But you better get up and get your ass inside, shift's about to start."

I wanted to explain to Angela that I wasn't *living* in my car, I was just temporarily sleeping in it. But she didn't care. She'd already started walking away. I glanced at my watch. It was five forty-five; I had fifteen minutes to spare. I pulled some clothes from the pile on the backseat and headed inside.

❧

It's hard to get comfortable in a car. Maybe if I was one of those little pint-sized gymnast types, it wouldn't have been so bad. But I'm a big girl and I need room to spread out. I tried all kinds of sleeping configurations: head in the backseat, legs splayed out over the headrests; head on the dashboard, hips in the air. But no matter how I positioned myself, the gearshift always seemed to end up in some part of my body not designed for hard objects.

I don't know what it is about a gearshift up your ass that gets you thinking about your future. *How am I ever going to meet Tito Jackson living like this?* I'd ask myself late into the night. And, *I sure miss watching* Wheel of Fortune. But mostly, I'd lie awake listening to Prince on my shitty car radio and dreading the day ahead.

As much as I hated being homeless, I had another problem on my hands that was making me feel even more hopeless: I hated working on the assembly line. Doing the same thing over and over hundreds of times a day was so damn boring, I felt like I was dying inside. But I didn't think I had any other options; I was sure this was going to be my life.

I'd grown up watching my mama work a string of low-wage hospital jobs and never get ahead. She was always scrambling just to keep the lights on. Seeing her struggle taught me that a job isn't supposed to be fun. I learned the way life goes is: (1) you get a job you hate; (2) you put in your time struggling and surviving; (3) if you're lucky, you get yourself an almost employed man. That's how Mama did it, and I assumed that's how I was supposed to live my life, too. After all, it wasn't just my mama who struggled; everyone at Brewster-Douglass who had a job seemed to hate it. They worked in day care centers or old-age homes, taking care of other people's families and cleaning up other people's mess. No one had a career they loved or a vocation that mattered to them. A job was just a way to put food on the table and sometimes it didn't even pay enough to do that.

Those nights alone in my car, I thought a lot about people, like Angela, who I met on the line. They worked twelve-, sometimes eighteen-hour shifts, six or seven days a week. And for what? The company had no loyalty. Everybody had a story about an old-timer who'd been with GM fifteen or twenty years and then suddenly got laid off, just like that. Nobody on the line seemed happy to be there. During lunch breaks, I saw people smoking crack in their cars and drinking liquor out of hip flasks they kept in their lockers. It seemed that getting high was the only way some folks could make it through the day.

Here I was, seventeen and homeless, worrying about whether I had what it took to keep installing window cranks and side-door carpet day in and day out. If I couldn't hack it at one of the best jobs the city had to offer, what was I going to do with my life?

❧

"Hold the line!" the foreman yelled.

I was hard at work one morning, a few months after Mama kicked me out, when suddenly everything on the assembly line ground to a halt. This was nothing new; things were always breaking down on the line—sometimes one of the links in the thick metal chains that held the car parts suspended in the air would break or an errant car part would get caught up in the conveyor belt and slow everything down. Other times, we didn't know what caused the line to stop. We would sit at our stations and wait for the engineers, who worked in fancy carpeted offices upstairs, to come down to the floor and figure out what was wrong.

Those unscheduled breaks could be ten minutes long or last for hours. You never knew. Most folks just sat there staring blankly into space until the line came back up. But I couldn't stand being bored so always brought along some-thing to read or a crossword from the newspaper to keep me occupied.

I picked up the thick paperback I'd brought with me that day. I'd found the book in the employee locker room, where someone had left it behind: *The Autobiography of Malcolm X as Told to Alex Haley.* Back then, I'd never heard of Malcolm X. Learning about civil rights revolutionaries wasn't part of the American History curriculum at my public school. But I recognized Alex Haley as the man who wrote *Roots,* which was turned into a made-for-TV movie that my mama invited her friends over to watch in 1977, when it first came on. It's the only time I saw my mother and her usually boisterous friends glued to the TV and not a single one of them was laughing.

I cracked open the book and began reading the first page of the introduction in which Alex Haley describes his impression of Malcolm X: "As a man, Malcolm X had the physical bearing and the inner self-confidence of a born aristocrat."

Aristocrat? What the hell is an aristocrat? I wondered. I made a mental note to look up the word later and continued reading: "No man in our time aroused such fear and hatred in the white man as did Malcolm, because in him the white man sensed an implacable foe."

Implacable foe? I glanced up, trying to remember if my pocket Webster's Dictionary was in the backseat of my car. I was going to need it if I was going to make my way past page 2 with all these big-ass words. I turned back to the book: "a man unreservedly committed to the cause of liberating the black man in American society..."

"*The Autobiography of Malcolm X!*" a voice boomed beside me. I turned to see a man in a crisp white button-down shirt, plaid necktie, and horn-rimmed glasses. I didn't know his name, but I'd seen him before. I'd noticed him because he dressed just like the engineers who came downstairs to fix the line when it stalled. Only this dude was black.

"That is a *great* book," he said, pointing to the paperback. "One of my favorites. I read it in college. How you liking it?"

I froze. This important-looking person was asking me to give him a book report and I hadn't even finished reading the first page. "Well," I started. "It's, uh, fascinating. Because, uh, Malcolm had the confidence of a born, um, *aristocrat.*"

"I know that's right!" said the man. "Malcolm *was* a king. That's a very astute observation, young lady." He looked around to make sure no one was watching, then he leaned in close and added in a near whisper, "By any means necessary, right?" As he spoke, he very discreetly clenched his fist in a Black Power salute, holding it behind his clipboard so only I could see.

"Yes, sir," I replied. I had no idea what the hell we were talking about! Who was this guy? He looked like a boss but was talking to me like maybe we were about to start a protest. Was I supposed to give him a Black Power salute in return? Did this mean I had joined The Revolution? That would definitely be a problem; I do not look good in an Afro. I tried to change the subject. "So, what do you do here?" I asked. "What's your job?"

"I'm Mr. Arnold," he replied, with a chuckle. "I'm an engineer. I work upstairs." He smiled. "And you are?"

"Loni," I said. "I glue carpet on the doors."

"It's a pleasure to make your acquaintance, Loni," he said. "It's not every day that I see someone on the line reading about Malcolm. I'm going to remember you."

"Thank you, sir," I said. "I'll be right here. With my glue gun, handling my business."

After that first meeting, every time I saw Mr. Arnold on the floor I'd give him a wave. Sometimes we'd get to chatting. He asked me how I'd done in high school (I told him math was my favorite subject) and if I liked the job (I told him I liked my paycheck). One day he asked me where I lived. I didn't want to tell him that I had recently moved out of the employee parking lot and was renting a room at the YWCA so I told him I lived at Brewster-Douglass, instead. A smile crept across his face.

"The playground still got that rickety swing set?" he asked.

"Yeah," I answered. "You been there?"

"Been there? Girl, I grew up there. Building 2 right behind the Shed."

"Get outta here!" I exclaimed. I didn't know any folks from the projects who wore collared shirts and dress shoes to work.

"Brewster-Douglass, born and bred!" Mr. Arnold said, and then, as though he was reading my mind, he added: "I bet you're wondering how I did all this." He waved his hand, gesturing to the assembly line as though he owned it.

"Yes, sir," I answered, lighting up. "I would love to know your story."

⌒

It wasn't a usual thing for engineers and line workers to spend much time talking. But I was fascinated by Mr. Arnold; there was something in my spirit that drew me to that man. I wanted to know his journey because I'd never heard anything like it before. "Interested" is how I felt at the time. But looking back, I see something different. I met Mr. Arnold when I was searching for answers. God sent him to show me the way.

Every couple of weeks, Mr. Arnold would invite me upstairs to his office, which was bigger than the apartment I grew up in, and we'd have lunch. Mr. Arnold would enjoy a cup of steaming coffee, which his assistant would bring. She'd hand me a sandwich wrapped in cellophane. I wondered if Mr. Arnold was sending his assistant out to the deli to buy me lunch. I felt bad for her but also jealous. Picking up lunch and making coffee seemed like a way better job than what I was doing.

Mr. Arnold told me that the key to his success was hard work and a good education. He said that the best schools in the world are HBCUs, which he explained stood for "historically black colleges and universities."

"Like Morehouse, Spelman, and Howard," he said. "Have you ever heard of those institutions?"

I hadn't.

"Those schools are where leaders are born," he continued. "They nurture brothers and sisters and prepare us to excel. I'm a Prairie View A&M man, myself," he added, telling me about the college located about fifty miles from Houston, Texas. "Prairie View has one of the best engineering programs in the country."

Mr. Arnold leaned back in his chair. On his desk was a framed picture of a woman I assumed was his wife, with two small children. They were standing in front of a white clapboard house with a neatly manicured lawn. In another picture, the kids were playing on a sandy beach. "Loni," he asked, peering out over his glasses. "Is college something you've ever thought about?"

"No, sir," I answered.

"Well," he said, leaning forward in his chair, "you should."

Mr. Arnold told me I had "promise," and that he respected my "determination" and "inquisitive mind."

"A good education will give you opportunities, Loni," he said. "This isn't only for your benefit. It's how we rise as a community. We've got to stick together. And it's the responsibility of brothers and sisters, like myself, who've risen above our circumstances to reach back and help another. I have a lot of contacts at Prairie View," he added. "If you are interested in college, I can help."

Mr. Arnold was the first person in my entire life to ever talk to me about college. My mother, who hadn't gone to college herself, certainly didn't mention it. Neither did any of my teachers at Cass Tech. Cass was supposed to be one of the best public high schools in the city of Detroit, but I never once met with a college counselor. I'm not even sure the school had one.

"You are college material," Mr. Arnold repeated as he walked me to his door. "Think it over."

I'll never forget how I felt the first time Mr. Arnold mentioned college; I thought he was crazy. Before I met Mr. Arnold, I didn't know anyone from Brewster-Douglass even went to college. But later that night, I began to wonder if maybe he was right. Maybe I *did* have what it takes to live a different kind of life. One that involves carpeted offices and fresh-brewed coffee instead of sleeping in my car.

For months, I had been ending my days praying to God to cover me so I would make it through the night alive. Survival was my number-one goal. But now, God was letting me know He had bigger plans for me. He'd sent me an angel in horn-rimmed glasses to deliver the message that it was time to change my life. All I had to do was listen.

Listen Up!

You never know when someone is going to bless you with their brilliance. Here are a few gems of wisdom I wasn't expecting but sure am glad I got:

"The people you meet on the way up are the same people you meet on the way down."
                —A crackhead trying to sell me a ladder

"Never take a break in Hollywood. When you need a break, Hollywood will give you one."
                                —Joan Rivers

"You better love yourself first because you may be the only one who ever will."
                —Miss French from Brewster-Douglass

CHAPTER 7

BREAKING UP
WITH MY BESTIE

The problem with not having a parent you can get advice from is you don't have anyone to turn to when it's time to make Big Life Decisions, like whether you should eat that tin of expired tunafish or if you should go to college. So, a few weeks after Mr. Arnold put the idea of higher education into my head, I dropped by Amber's house to see what her mama had to say about the plan. After all, Ms. Davis was one of the only people I knew who'd actually gone to college. She had a two-year associate's degree in business administration, which she never let anyone forget.

"So, I've been talking to a man at the GM plant," I began, "about my future. He's an engineer and he said he could help me get ahead in life."

"Oh, Loni," Ms. Davis said with a sigh. "You are such a bright girl. You don't need to spend time with the management to get ahead." She raised her fingers and made air quotes when she said "get ahead." I didn't know what the hell that was supposed to mean. I glanced over at Amber, but she just shrugged.

It had been months since I had last seen my best friend. I was busy living that GM life and Amber, who was a year younger than me, was still in high school. I noticed she'd painted her nails the same cherry red polish as her mother had, and she was wearing matching lipstick. I'd never seen Amber in makeup before. I tugged at my faded T-shirt, wishing I'd worn something nicer.

"You have to be careful, Loni," Ms. Davis continued. "Sometimes older men see a young woman at the workplace and they get certain...ideas."

"Oh my God!" Amber interrupted, with a snort. "Mama thinks your boss wants to hit it! Like, he's gonna help you climb the GM ladder if you give him some booty."

"Oh, hell no!" I objected. "Mr. Arnold is married. He has a *wife*! It's not even like that."

"Then what, exactly, are the two of you talking about?" Ms. Davis asked. She folded her arms in front of her chest and stared at me expectantly.

I suddenly wished I'd never come over. Ever since we were little, I'd kept my personal business to myself. I didn't tell Amber and her mother about the times Mama's lights got turned off or when we ran out of groceries. I would simply go over to Amber's house, hang out, do homework, read magazines, and eat her mama's snacks. Ms. Davis didn't even know I was staying at the YWCA. So, what was I thinking asking her about the biggest decision of my life? What if Ms. Davis laughed at me and told me to stay in my lane? What if she said college was for other people?

"So?" Amber prompted. "What's up?"

I took a breath and with my eyes glued to the floor, I told

them everything. I told them about reading *Malcolm X* and Mr. Arnold inviting me to his office; I repeated what he'd said about Prairie View being a good school and how he could help me get in. I told them Mr. Arnold had suggested I major in engineering. "Because I like math," I added lamely. "But never mind. It's a stupid idea."

Ms. Davis stared into space for a long time, as if she was putting together a puzzle in her head. "You know," she said finally, "this might be perfect."

Ms. Davis explained that she was planning for Amber to go to college next fall, too. If we both went to Prairie View, she said, I could look out for her daughter. "It's going to be Amber's first time away from home," she added. "If you were with her, I'd know she'd be taken care of."

She could count on me, I assured her. Amber and I had been ride-or-die since Bible study summer camp. "I've got Amber's back," I said.

I'd been so worried to talk to Amber's mama about college, but in the end she turned out to be almost as supportive as Mr. Arnold. She helped me with my application and studying for the SAT. In return, I pledged to look out for her daughter when we both got our acceptance letters from Prairie View later that spring. What I didn't know at the time was that I was making a promise that would be very hard to keep.

It turns out that Amber and I had very different college-student goals. I wanted to get good grades. Amber, on the other hand, seemed like she was on a mission to get her some Ds. And not just on her report card.

We'd been at college for less than a week when Amber got herself invited to her first fraternity party. "It's gonna be sooooooo dope!" she squealed, bouncing into our dorm room. "Girl, this isn't just any frat party," she added. "It's a Kappa party."

At Prairie View, every fraternity had its own flavor, style, and claim to fame. The Kappa Alpha Psis were known as the "pretty boys." They all had super-long eyelashes and bright white Colgate smiles. Then there were the brothers in Alpha Phi Alpha. That frat was legendary for attracting the smartest boys on campus—Thurgood Marshall and Martin Luther King were Alphas. The boys from Phi Beta Sigma threw the best parties. But by far, the most badass fraternity at Prairie View was Omega Psi Phis. Those brothers called themselves Q Dogs, Ques, or Omega Men, and, if you were into rugged dudes who liked to party, you'd be all up in that mess.

To really understand the vibe of each frat, all you had to do was watch a step show. Prairie View is an HBCU, so of course we had some of the best step shows on the planet! The Ques stepped in camouflage cargos and Timberland boots, looking like they were ready for combat. Sometimes, in midroutine, they'd tear off their shirts and hump the stage. Meanwhile, the Kappas kept it classy. They'd do their step choreography in crisp white shirts, red bow ties, and with their trademark red-and-white canes. The way a lot of girls saw it: Ques were bad boys; Kappas were boyfriend material.

"Franklin's gonna be there," Amber gushed about one of the most popular Kappas on campus. "So, I need to look *extra* juicy."

Every freshman girl wanted a piece of Franklin. With his light skin, wavy hair, and green eyes, he looked like what would happen if Idris Elba and Brad Pitt had a baby. I wanted to tell Amber to lower her expectations. But instead I bit my tongue and watched as she reached into her giant pink suitcase—which she still hadn't bothered to unpack—and started flinging clothes onto her bed.

"What do you think?" she asked, holding a black leather belt against her hips.

"It's all right."

She picked up a white off-the-shoulder top. "I could wear it with this," she said. She grabbed a pair of patent leather pumps. "And these."

"Sure," I replied. "But what are you wearing on the bottom? Jeans or a skirt?"

Amber looked at me quizzically. She pointed to the belt. "That *is* a skirt," she said. "It's a mini. A micro mini."

Amber pressed the skirt-belt to her hips and twisted around so she was looking at her backside in the mirror. Then she bent over and shook her booty. "Oh, I know just the thing," she said, standing up. From the mess of clothes in her suitcase Amber fished out a pair of lacy, high-cut black panties. "I got them at Victoria's Secret," she said, holding them up. "Sexy, right?"

I had never shopped at Victoria's Secret before. I bought my panties in packs of six from the dollar store. Furthermore, I wasn't sure why Amber needed high-cut sexy panties...that is, unless she was planning an evening of showing them off. I had planned to spend the evening studying, but suddenly it occurred to me that Amber looking "extra juicy" at a frat party was exactly the type of situation Ms. Davis had asked me to prevent.

"I'm coming with you," I announced, hopping down from my bunk.

Amber tilted her head to the side, giving me the once-over. "If you're coming," she said, "you need to look cute."

Unlike my bestie—who'd brought three suitcases full of clothes—I'd brought only one duffel bag. Mr. Arnold had given it to me as a going-away gift, and I had filled it with faded T-shirts and jeans; the black slacks and white button-down shirt I'd worn to my high school orchestra recitals; and my lavender prom dress, because you never know when you might get invited to a ball.

"I don't have anything like that," I said, pointing to Amber's skirt-belt, unplanned pregnancy ensemble.

"You didn't bring *nothing* nice?" she asked, sounding irritated.

I reached into my bottom dresser drawer and pulled out my prom dress. "I do have this," I said, holding it to my chest. The dress billowed around me in clouds of lace and tulle.

Amber's eyes grew wide as she raised her hand to cover her gaping mouth. I thought for a second she was going to bust out laughing. Instead, she cleared her throat and pointed to my dress. "Yes, girl," she said. "Definitely wear that."

Looking back, I realize that was the first sign that my relationship with Amber wasn't what I thought. There is one rule of friendship that every woman knows: you are not, under any circumstances, allowed to let your best friend go to a party looking a hot-ass mess. Every good friend knows this. It's in the best-friend bylaws: *Thou shall not let thou's girlfriend play herself wearing that avocado-green jumpsuit that looked good on her twenty pounds ago.* And you are definitely not supposed to make sure your friend wears an outfit that makes YOU look good. But that's exactly what Amber was up to. We left the dorm with her looking like a member of En Vogue and me looking like Tyler Perry in *Medea's Family Reunion*.

In the end, it didn't even matter what I wore because as soon as we got to the party Amber threw back five shots of a drink the boys called "sex juice," which was made of 190-proof Everclear, grape Kool-Aid, and ice cubes in a giant plastic bowl. I spent the rest of the night saving Amber from her drunk-ass self.

I pulled her out of a boy's dorm room, where she was bent over with her Vicky's Secrets on full display. Then I yanked her off a sofa just as she was about to get into a tongues-out make-out sesh with a Kappa that I knew was somebody else's guy. Then I wrestled her to the ground on the dance floor to keep her from becoming the girl meat in the middle of a frat boy sandwich.

At two o'clock in the morning, she passed out on the lawn. I picked her up, threw her over my shoulder like a fireman would, and carried her back to our dorm, where she promptly threw up all over her pink and white Laura Ashley comforter.

The next afternoon, when she finally stumbled out of bed, I was expecting Amber to hang her head in shame. I thought for sure she'd thank me for taking care of her and apologize to me for acting so crazy. But all she had to say for herself was, "That was so cool!"

Cool?

This was *not* my idea of a "cool" time, not at all. When I was in high school, my social life consisted of singing along to a record at the Jehovah's Witness Kingdom Hall, going to orchestra practice, and running my Brewster-Douglass grocery delivery business ("For All Your Shopping Needs!"). I wasn't about that underage-binge-drinking lifestyle. But Amber couldn't get enough. It was like sharing a dorm room with Snoop Dogg.

Before too long, Amber and I slid into a routine: During the week, I'd wake her up, make sure she made it to class on time, and remind her to call her mother. On weekends, she'd go out and have too much fun. Then I'd drag her home and clean her up. I didn't feel like Amber's best friend anymore; I felt like her unpaid and unappreciated personal assistant. And not once did she thank me. In fact, just the opposite. Amber started making fun of me. She called me "little old lady" and "big ole nerd."

But still, I hung in there. I thought maybe she was going through a phase. Until she came back to her senses, I reasoned, I had to keep her safe and in school. I worried about Amber getting to class on time. I worried about her when she snuck out at night. I worried about the fact I didn't have proper first aid training to deal with possible alcohol poisoning or STDs. I worried I was failing at the promise I'd made Amber's mama and that I was letting Amber down.

I was on 24/7 Amber Alert and the stress was killing me. I wasn't sleeping, I had a headache all the time, I lost my appetite . . . well, okay, I didn't lose my appetite, but you get the idea. What I didn't realize, until it was almost too late, was that the whole time I was worried about Amber I should have been focusing on my own damn self.

❧

College is a time to learn life lessons, and here's one of the first lessons I learned: college is hella expensive!

When I left Detroit and headed to Prairie View, I had $6,500 in savings I'd put away from my General Motors job. It felt like a fortune, like I was ballin'. But it was nowhere near enough to pay for four years of college education.

In all my pre-college talks with Mr. Arnold, somehow we missed this part. Or maybe he talked to me about it, but it didn't sink in. Or maybe he figured I was from Brewster-Douglass and had that survivor instinct, so once I got to school, I'd find the money somehow. But coming up with college money isn't like snatching a book of food stamps out of your granny's bra. I didn't know anything about applying for financial aid or how to get a loan. I didn't have a dollar *or* a plan.

I was dead-ass broke.

I know what you're thinking: *everyone is broke in college*. But not all broke is the same. I grew up in a certain type of poverty. At Brewster-Douglass, we were wash-your-clothes-in-the-bathtub-because-you-don't-have-quarters-for-the-laundromat poor. We were ketchup-sandwiches-for-dinner poor. We were Mama-ain't-got-money-for-Christmas-presents poor.

It didn't occur to me until I got to college that when other people said they didn't have any money, they meant something else entirely. At Prairie View, I heard other kids complain they were "broke" all the time, and yet these same kids still had money for books and food and paying tuition. It's like they had access to some kind of secret emergency fund that I didn't know about. I came to learn that this secret fund was called "parents."

Not every kid at Prairie View was well-off, but most of them had home addresses and people who cared for them. My last address was the backseat of my car. And when I called my mama collect from the land line in my dorm to tell her how I was doing, she told me not to phone so much because I was running up her bill. I had nobody looking out for me and nothing to fall back on. I had to handle everything on my own.

I spent a lot of time scouring the school's job boards looking for moneymaking opportunities. I was able to cobble together a few gigs to make me some extra cash. I got a part-time job playing the French horn for the school band during football game intermissions that paid $100 per gig and I made $7.50 an hour working for a local gas station giving out flyers advertising their new car wash. When money was really tight, I could donate blood plasma for $25 plus free cookies and juice. Once I even volunteered for a medical experiment. I made $150 and got a rash that took two weeks to go away. But all this was just pocket money. It still wasn't enough to pay for my tuition and housing.

And then, just as I was beginning to think my college dreams were over, God came through. Not once, but twice! First, I got a call from my advisor telling me he needed to see me. I couldn't imagine why. I'd been studying my ass off and had the grades to prove it, all As and one B. But it turned out, my advisor had good news to share. He'd submitted my name for a scholarship, and I'd won! I was going to be an official General Motors Scholar, and GM was going to pay my tuition until graduation. I couldn't believe the company I used to work for was sponsoring the scholarship. Suddenly, I felt real bad about all the carpeting I'd glued on crooked while I was working in the plant.

I found the solution to my housing crisis a few weeks later as I was scanning the job board looking for a new medical experiment that might pay me some money.

And then, one afternoon while I was scanning the job board, I found the answer to my prayers: a flyer looking for a resident adviser for one of the freshman girls' dorms. "Applicants must be mature, dependable, responsible, and with excellent communication skills," the flyer said. The job entailed acting as a big sister to a dorm of incoming freshmen, keeping them out of trouble, and helping them adjust to college life. It paid a small weekly stipend plus free dorm and board.

I applied for the position, highlighting my experience as a sober living coach and unplanned pregnancy preventer, and I got the job. With my scholarship in place and my housing crisis averted, everything was finally coming together. Everything except Amber.

Amber was my best friend. But taking care of her was killing me. After a lot of sleepless nights, it finally dawned on me: I had to let her go.

∼

I used to think loyalty was the most important quality in a friendship. Growing up without a mother I could depend on made me hang on tight to my friends. But I've come to learn that friendships are like house parties: once they are over you don't want to stick around.

I'd known for months that Amber and I were growing apart. We didn't like the same things or have the same priorities. And I knew she didn't appreciate me for who I was—a mature, responsible friend who'd never let her down. But the final blow to our relationship came when I discovered the loyalty that I thought I shared with Amber was a one-way street.

It was the end of freshman year. I needed to pick up a copy of Toni Morrison's *The Bluest Eye* for English class, but all the copies in the library were out and I was short the $4.99 I needed to buy the paperback at the school's bookstore. I had exactly thirty-seven cents to my name. I was desperate.

"Can I borrow four dollars and sixty-two cents?" I asked Amber. I told her I'd pay her back by the end of the week, after I hit up the blood bank and made a plasma donation. "I'll even get you some of those free cookies they give out at the clinic," I said.

Amber pretended not to hear me. She was peering into her hand mirror and rubbing gloss on her lips.

"Amber," I said again. "Please..."

"Whatever," she finally answered, with a snort. She reached into her wallet and took out a five-dollar bill. But instead of handing it to me, like a normal person, she crumpled it up and threw it on the ground. "You *better* pay me back," she said. Then she stormed out of the room. I felt like I'd been slapped in the face.

I had spent almost an entire school year dragging Amber home from parties and waking her up for class. I couldn't believe this was how she treated me in return.

I want to say I broke up with Amber after that incident. And I really want to tell you I did it in a mature and dignified way. Like, I sat her down over a cup of tea and said, "This isn't working out. It's you, not me."

But I was just a kid, and I still had a lot of growing up to do. I wouldn't learn to be direct and up-front until later in life. Instead, I did what most people do when they want to get out of a relationship but don't have the nerve to confront the other person: I ghosted her. Only this was before cell phones and tech made ghosting easy. I had to ghost Amber the old-fashioned way. I had to run and hide. I transferred into another dorm and spent the last month of freshman year ducking and weaving every time I saw Amber coming my way. I hid behind potted plants, trees in the quad, and the occasional football player. But it was all worth it. Sophomore year, I returned to Prairie View without a bestie who treated me like a servant. Instead, I had a brand-new babysitting job watching over a dorm full of girls.

It turns out all the qualities that made me a "little old lady nerd" in Amber's eyes made me the best RA Prairie View had ever seen. I was no-nonsense and big on rules. I comforted girls when they were feeling homesick; showed them all the different ways you can cook potatoes; and dispensed sex ed advice, even though I barely knew anything about it myself. When one girl asked me to explain what 69 meant, I told her it's a multiple of three. When another girl forgot to take her birth control pills for a few days, then devoured the entire pack "as a precaution," I was the one who took her to the hospital.

But of all my caretaking duties, the most important, by far, was making sure all boys were out of the dorm by the midnight curfew. Lucky for me, all those years playing French horn had given me excellent breath control. When I stood at the top of the hall and yelled, "VISITING HOURS ARE OVER!" dudes would scatter like a bunch of Brewster-Douglass cockroaches when the kitchen lights come on. Sometimes they'd exit so fast, they'd leave some of their possessions behind. That's how I ended up with a satin Raiders starter jacket and a pair of Nike Air Force 1s.

After a year of struggling as Amber's college crisis manager, I finally found my place at Prairie View. I wasn't a party girl or a nerd. I wasn't even the girl from the projects struggling to get by. I claimed my crown as the trusted Big Sister and most reliable girl on campus. Not everyone can be the life of the party. Someone has to be sober and in charge.

Without Amber to take care of, I was finally able to focus on *me*. I discovered a whole world of things I could do on Saturday nights besides sitting on the floor of the girls' bathroom holding Amber's weave out of the toilet. I pledged Delta Sigma Theta sorority, I excelled in my engineering classes, and I produced and starred in an on-campus one-woman production called *The Wanda Winfrey Show*. The premise was that Wanda was Oprah's little sister who ran a talk show in the Student Center. Just like her big sis, Wanda addressed pressing issues of the day, like the origins of the suspicious meat served in the dining hall. That show was my baby. I came up with the idea, booked the guests—the cafeteria lady was a big draw—and worked the room like a pro, taking questions from the audience and cracking all kinds of jokes.

Every time I left the stage at the Student Center, it was like the Junior Talent Show all over again. The feeling of fireworks in my stomach, the satisfaction I felt at making folks laugh—it all came rushing back. Getting reacquainted with my passion for performing wasn't what I expected when I ended my relationship with Amber. But it just goes to show you, if the person you're holding on to the tightest is the one holding you back, it's time to let them go.

You Know Your Friendship's Over When...

- Every time she calls, you send it to voicemail, and you never check your voicemail.
- She invites you to her parents' house for dinner and you agree to go, but only if she won't be there.
- You spend a Sunday afternoon scrolling backward through Instagram just so you can unlike all her pics.
- You read her Facebook posts and find yourself screaming at your computer, "Your baby is ugly!"
- You purposely buy an Android phone so she can't FaceTime you.
- You pray her new relationship works out so she will leave you the hell alone.

CHAPTER 8

THE HIGH PRICE OF WRONG ASSUMPTIONS

Sometimes you just know you look good. So good, nobody can't tell you nothin'. That's how I felt one Friday night during my senior year at Prairie View, when my friend Keisha and I decided to hit the club. We were both working as weekend cashiers in a grocery store in downtown Houston. The plan was, we would change into our going-out clothes in the employee restroom, then spend the night getting our swerve on before Keisha drove us the forty-minute ride back to campus.

"Check this out," Keisha said excitedly, busting out her best booty-poppin' imitation of the girls in the Wreckx-N-Effect "Rump Shaker" video as we got ready in the ladies' room after work.

"All I wanna do is zoom-a-zoom-zoom-zoom," I sang, busting a few moves of my own. I still wasn't much of a dancer. But Just like when I was little and competed in the Junior Talent Show, what I lacked in skills I made up for in presentation. That night I was rocking my most show-stopping outfit: a pair of billowy black-and-white cheetah-print, three-quarter-length parachute pants paired with an off-the-shoulder asymmetrical white satin tank top, perfectly matched to my asymmetrical bob. I finished off the ensemble with gold-plated giant hoop earrings and a pair of electric-blue fake crocodile embossed pleather pumps. I was serving *all* the looks: MC Hammer on the bottom and Salt-N-Pepa up top.

Keisha and I had a ball that night, tearing up the dance floor and closing down the club. It was two a.m. when we finally stumbled out of there, with our feet on fire. Maybe if we had headed back to school right then, like we'd planned, the night would have turned out fine. But, instead, we decided to stop for a quick bite to eat at Jose's, an all-night Mexican restaurant. That's when everything started to go wrong.

I was at the cashier paying for my chicken chimichanga when, from the corner of my eye, I caught sight of a commotion. Keisha, who'd gone ahead of me in line, was getting yanked away from the soda machine by a red-faced cop who looked just like Dan, the meaty-armed, potbellied husband from *Roseanne*. He had Keisha by her upper arm and was pulling her toward the swinging doors of the kitchen.

"Keisha," I called out. "You okay?"

She looked at me with terrified eyes. I left my tray at the counter and ran after them, pushing my way through the crowd of people who'd turned to stare, and barging into the kitchen.

The cop had pushed Keisha up against the wall and was handcuffing her wrists behind her back.

"What's going on?" I asked, trying to sound calm.

"Ain't none of your damn business," the officer barked in a gruff southern accent that put me on edge.

"But I *know* her," I insisted. "She's my ride. We go to Prairie View. We have to get back to school."

"I don't give a shit where you gotta be," he said. "Your little friend here is under arrest."

"But I didn't do nothing," Keisha wailed.

"That right?" sneered the cop. "Because I saw you fill up a water cup with soda. You didn't pay for it. That's what I call theft."

Jose's was set up cafeteria-style, so you'd take a tray and get your food at a service line. At the end of the counter, past the cashiers, was a drink machine where you'd fill up your cup with water or soda depending on what you'd paid for. If you paid for soda, the cashier would give you a clear cup. If you asked for water—which was free—you'd get a green cup. Apparently, Keisha had tried to pull a fast one filling up her water cup with soda. Now we were in this hot-ass mess.

"Sir," Keisha said, "it was a mistake! I swear."

"Mistake my ass," said the cop.

I couldn't blame him. Even I knew Keisha was lying. Still, I tried to intervene: "Sir, you can't arrest a person for stealing a cup of soda. It's, like, a *dollar*. What are you going to charge her with—soda robbery in the first degree?"

The officer swung around to face me. "I've had about enough of your fucking attitude. You think I don't see how you people are always trying to get something for nothing? Turn around," he demanded. "You're under arrest, too."

I stood there, stunned, sure I must have misheard him. He pulled from his side pocket another pair of handcuffs: "TURN THE FUCK AROUND."

Slowly, I raised my hands in the air, like I'd seen on TV.

"Why are you arresting *me*?" I asked. "All I did was come in here to check on my friend."

"This here is private property. You're trespassing. Both you nigger bitches is going to jail. Now close your fucking mouth before I close it for you."

It felt like everything was moving in slow motion, my brain scrambling to make sense of it all. *Did this motherfucker just call me the N-word? I thought. And is he SERIOUSLY taking my ass to jail?* I opened my mouth to politely ask him what in the actual fuck his problem was. But before I could get a word out, he'd spun me around by my shoulder, clamped the handcuffs on my wrists, and shoved me hard against the wall.

"You have the right to remain silent," he began.

From the corner of my eye, I caught sight of one of the kitchen staff who was frozen in place, holding a head of lettuce and watching the scene unfold. "Help me," I mouthed in his direction. "*Por favor!*" But he didn't move. He looked even more scared than I felt.

A few minutes later, two more officers arrived on the scene to take us back to the station for processing. As they loaded us into the back of their patrol car, I tried to explain this had all been a mistake. "Officer," I said to the one nearest me. "I didn't do anything."

He gave me a look of sheer disgust, like I was something he'd found on the bottom of his shoe. Nobody had ever looked at me like that before. And most definitely not when I was dressed in my flowy cheetah pants. "I mean it," I said. "I'm innocent."

"Right," he snorted, putting his hand on the top of my head and pushing me into the car. "That's what they all say."

The officers drove us to the local precinct. It was the last time I'd see Keisha that night.

It turns out that stealing a cup of soda is a misdemeanor. But my crime of "trespassing" was a felony. I was ushered to a different part of the building, where the serious criminals were kept.

I got fingerprinted and strip-searched, which is as bad as it sounds. A female officer told me to take down my pants and spread my cheeks. "Let me know if you find my missing house keys down there," I said, bending over. She didn't even laugh.

On the way to the women's holding cell, I passed a line of about a dozen black men of varying ages, builds, and complexions handcuffed hands behind their backs and shackled at the ankles. Seeing those brothers huddled together, with their heads hung low, I was reminded of a scene from *Roots*. It had stunned me to see black men chained like animals on television, and it shocked me even more to see it in real life.

"Keep it moving," a police officer yelled. I looked away from the men and continued down the corridor. At the end of the hall, I was put in a cage with half a dozen other black women who'd been arrested that night.

⟡

Before my arrest, I didn't know anything about jail. And I sure as hell didn't expect it to be a place I'd ever make friends. But as soon as the officer pushed me into the cell, I met Beulah, a very large middle-aged woman wearing a faded nightgown and rollers in her hair. Beulah looked up and gave me a big, wide-open smile. "What up, bitch?" she said. "I sure like them fancy pants you got on!"

Beulah, who was one of eight women already in the holding cell, explained she was dressed in her night clothes because the "muthafuckin po po" had pulled her out of bed in the middle of the night and arrested her for writing bad checks. "That's how they do!" she said. "Get you when you most vulnerable. I know one dude, this brother was yanked right off the toilet! These fuckers don't give a shit how they treat no-fucking-body." She shook her head.

This wasn't Beulah's first time behind bars. She was an OG at county jail, she said, matter-of-factly. Because of her vast experience in the criminal justice system, Beula quickly became the self-appointed jailhouse counsel dispensing legal advice to our entire incarcerated group. First up was Chantelle, who'd gotten beaten by the cops when they'd stopped her for a speeding violation and discovered she had a bunch of outstanding warrants. She asked Beulah if she could sue the city for the black eye and split lip the cops had inflicted upon her. "Shiiii-iiiit, it's your word against the cops'," Beulah said. "You know good and goddamn well that's a losing case right there."

Then came Diane, a freshman at the University of Houston who had been caught up in a drug bust when the cops raided her boyfriend's apartment. "I didn't even know he sold drugs until the police broke down his door," she said.

Beulah told Diane she needed to get herself a lawyer and that if her boyfriend was any good at drug dealing, he'd pay for it himself. "That's what a real muthafucka that love you would do," she said.

Roxanne was pregnant and looked to be around my age.

Earlier that night she had shot her baby-daddy in the leg in self-defense. Rubbing her pregnant belly, she told us that her man had threatened to blow her head off. "I just got to the gun first," Roxanne said. "Now they got me up in here for attempted murder."

"Girl, what you shoulda done," said Beulah, "is shot that nigga square in the balls. Blow them shits right off that muthafucka. Now that would have been some real justice, you feel me? I hope the judge don't make you have that baby in prison, though."

When it was my turn for free legal advice, I told Beulah all about Keisha's soda robbery and my trespassing charge. The entire holding cell erupted in laughter. I'm pretty sure the cops at the end of the hall who overheard my story cracked up, too.

"That's some straight bullshit!" Beulah said. "Girl, you don't even need to worry. The judge is gonna throw that charge right out."

"When?" I asked. "I need to leave. I have to study for my electronics exam."

"Sis, what you *need* to do is calm your ass down because we're gonna be here for a while," she replied. "You won't see a judge until Monday morning at the soonest."

My pulse quickened. Monday was three days away. "I can't stay in here that long," I said. "I just . . . I can't."

Beulah just laughed. "You'll be a'ight," she said. Then, without missing a beat, she proceeded to tell me of all the horrors I had in store. In a few hours we would be transferred to central booking, she explained. We'd be issued orange jumpsuits to change into. "But before they let you put on the jumpsuit," she said, "they're gonna strip you down and do a full body inspection."

"No," I interjected. "I already got searched."

"Bitch, please," she said. "That was a precinct search. I'm talking about central booking and they don't play. They gonna do a deep dive into *all* your cavities. After that, they hose you off with water, up, down, and all around. Like a goddam car wash." Only then, Beulah said, would I be moved to a cell. "That's when you get chosen," she added.

"Chosen for what?" I asked, picturing high school gym class. "Do they have teams?"

Beulah let out a whoop. "Girl, you really don't know shit," she said through her laughter. "Some of them girls at central booking been locked up a good long time. They waiting for the new bitches so they can get boo'ed up. Everybody wants somebody to snuggle with, you know what I'm saying. Or . . . whatever." Beulah took one look at the horror on my face and started laughing even louder. "They really gonna like you."

"Oh no, ma'am!" I said, shaking my head. "That is *not* happening."

"Then you best find somebody to bail you out," Beulah advised. "You got parents you can call?"

I shook my head no.

"Well, you better think of somebody. Or else you're here for the weekend, with the rest of us."

Somehow Beulah, who was only trying to help, had managed to make me even more terrified than I was when I first walked into the cell. I started banging on the bars, hollering to the officer at the end of the hall. "Please," I begged. "It's an emergency. I need to make a call."

⌒

Six Things That Will Get You Arrested—But Only If You're Black

- Wearing socks in the swimming pool
- Strolling in the park trying to enjoy a beautiful day
- Shopping for a designer belt at Barneys
- Driving your own car
- Running from the sound of gunfire
- Cooperating with the police

I don't know a single black person who can't remember the first time they got a taste of being treated differently because of the color of their skin. It's a defining moment you never forget. Maybe it's when you got called the N-word on the playground or got followed around a store by a suspicious clerk. For me, I didn't feel racism slap me in the face until the night that power-tripping white police officer threw my ass in jail.

Of course, growing up, the effects of racism were all around me—racism is how Detroit got its segregated housing, underfunded public schools, and overaggressive cops—but as a kid, I didn't feel personally attacked. At Brewster-Douglass, Cass Tech, General Motors, and Prairie View, I'd been enveloped in cocoons of blackness, surrounded by people who looked like me. For my whole life I'd only ever been judged as a complete person—based on my behavior, accomplishments, or character—and never solely because of my race.

I was a good girl; anybody who spent any time with me knew that. The most sassy thing I'd ever done in life may have been buying those cheetah pants. I knew there were police that threw innocent black people behind bars, but before that night I didn't think it would ever happen to me. Sitting in that jail cell, it dawned on me that the cop at the Mexican restaurant would not have arrested a white boy who made the mistake of hanging out with an accused soda thief. He wouldn't have put me in handcuffs if I'd looked like his son.

It didn't matter if I was innocent. The cops at the precinct weren't going to let me go. If I wanted to get out of that jail cell, I had to get some outside help. I didn't have parents who could bail me out, but I did have people I could call. The year before, I'd become a member of the Delta Sigma Theta sorority, one of the oldest black sororities in Greek life. At Prairie View, the Deltas were known as the smart girls, the determined girls, the ones who *got shit done*. And I definitely had a lot of shit that needed to get done that night.

When the officer finally took me out of the cage to use the pay phone to make my one call, I dialed the number of a sorority sister I'd pledged with, my line sister, Dawn. After five rings, and what felt like an eternity, I finally heard her groggy voice on the other end of the line. I was so relieved, I started to cry. "I need help," I told her through sobs. "I'm wearing my cheetah pants..."

"Slow down," she said. "Start from the beginning."

I took a breath and told her everything. She responded with

the sweetest words I've ever heard: "Don't worry. We got you. We're gonna get you out."

I hung up feeling hopeful for the first time that night. But the feeling didn't last. As soon as I got back to the cell, I found out we were moving. Everyone in the holding cell was handcuffed and shackled together. We were marched down a long corridor and outside to a fenced-in area at the back of the building where we were loaded into the back of a paddy wagon.

"Where are they taking us?" I asked Beulah.

"Central booking," she replied. I was terrified that Dawn, who was on her way to the precinct, would never find me, and I was even more worried I would get "chosen" before she did.

We drove more than half an hour before I finally felt the vehicle come to a stop. We were led into a large building and brought to a cinder-block room with a heavy steel door that an officer locked from the outside. All I could think was, *If there's a fire, we're all going to die.*

I leaned my head back against the wall, closed my eyes, and tried to stay calm. My deep breathing must have worked because for the first time that night I dozed off.

I woke up to the sound of a heavy metal clank. A cop was unlocking the cell door and sliding a stack of cardboard trays on the ground. "Eat up," he said, closing the door behind him. He'd brought lunch. It was the first food I'd seen since getting locked up almost ten hours earlier. I suddenly realized I was starving.

I've had some horrible meals in my life—most of them involving potatoes—but nothing compared to this. There was a scoop of grayish mush that, based on the texture, I guessed was canned corn, a slice of slimy meat—possibly ham, but I couldn't be sure—a piece of dried-out white bread, and a small container of warm milk that had expired two days earlier. I pushed away the tray without touching a thing.

"You better eat something," Beulah said. "We gonna be here for a while."

"No," I insisted. "My people are coming for me."

I spent another three hours in that hellhole—praying I wouldn't get taken upstairs to be inspected, hosed down, and turned into some chick's jailhouse boo—before I finally got the news I'd been hoping for for hours: "Love!" an officer called, leaning into the cell. "You're getting out."

Beulah let out a whoop of congratulations. "Bitch, your people came through!"

Except for the time I got my test results at the free clinic after my friend Rhonda's ho-for-a-night-themed bachelorette party, I've never felt so good. I jumped up from the bench and started saying my farewells. Even though we'd only been locked up together for less than a day, these ladies were like family.

"Beulah," I said, giving her a hug, "you take care of yourself and stop writing those bad checks! Roxanne, you keep your head up! Chantelle, girl, you need to take care of those outstanding warrants and obey the speed limit. Diane, cut that drug dealer loose. You deserve better!"

Two weeks later, I showed up for my court appearance. Just as Beulah had predicted, the trespassing charge was thrown out. Eventually, it was expunged from my record, as well. But the memory of that night will always haunt me. I'd grown up in the projects, which is supposed to be one of the worst places to live in America. But the whole time I'd lived in Brewster-Douglass,

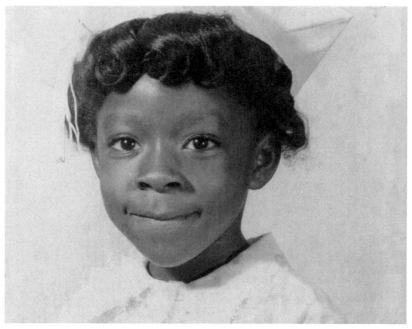

This is me at my most innocent, in my kindergarten graduation photo. Yes,
I did my own hair and makeup that day.

Middle school picture day had me going for that young astronaut look.

The famous Brewster Wheeler Recreation Center, where all the magic began.

This photo of me at fifteen holds a special place in my heart. Not only did I sew the suit myself, this is also the last time I could cross my legs.

At my high school graduation, I thanked all the folks at Brewster–Douglass who'd made the day possible, including the senior citizens who paid me to deliver their groceries and the drug dealers who *didn't* sell me crack.

At home celebrating high school graduation with my biggest fan at the time, the sad clown in the velvet painting behind me.

I love this picture of Diana Ross and The Supremes with the Brewster-Douglass towers looming behind them. When I was a kid, Diana and the ladies used to drive through the projects and wave to us from the backseat of their limousine. They made us all so proud and gave us hope for a better life ahead. (Detroit News Archive)

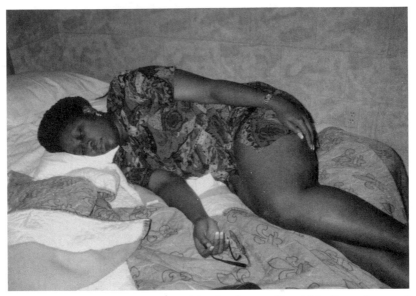

Doesn't everybody have a picture like this from college? No, I wasn't passed out drunk! I was taking a much-needed "study break." Statistics always put me in a coma.

Look out world! Here I am working the stage at Prairie View's student center like a boss rehearsing my "Wanda Winfrey Show." This was the first step in my stand-up life.

Here I am working hard as a young engineer in my pre-wig days. I look like I'm enjoying that cubicle life but really, I'm secretly writing jokes about my coworkers.

Here I am in the late 90s. After putting in long hours as an engineer at Xerox, the only thing that put a smile on my face was hearing folks laugh at my jokes about Bob from accounting.

This is my first official head shot, from 2002. As you can see, I had yet to discover the magic of fake eyelashes.

I made my national TV debut on *Star Search,* in 2003. Here I am with host Arsenio Hall. I had big dreams, but I still kept my day job. The morning after this pic was taken, I was back at my cubicle at Xerox.

This is me in 2004 with my manager Judi Marmel, the woman who helped change my life—and not just by loaning me money!

After I left my full-time job at Xerox, I booked my first appearance on the *Tonight Show* in 2005. Yes, I rocked the same suit I wore on *Star Search*. But I zhushed it up by adding the scarf. It's the little details that count (especially when you're too broke to buy a new outfit).

This is me and James enjoying a night on the town in 2019. He's my best friend, my plus one, and my designated driver.

I finally got to meet Tito Jackson. Dreams really do come true!

I never felt as afraid and disrespected as I did in the presence of that one racist cop. I wouldn't wish that feeling on anyone.

I experienced some hard truths that night: I learned that the color of my skin meant I wasn't going to get the same friends-and-family pass that most white folks got. And I learned that once I stepped outside the cocoon of blackness that had sheltered me all my life, I was at the mercy of anyone in power who might take one look at me, see a black woman, and make assumptions about who I am and what I'm all about.

A few years later, when I entered the cutthroat world of show business, where I had to deal with all kinds of industry prejudice, I was prepared. Once you've been caged for being the "wrong" color in the wrong place at the wrong time—and discovered that even in the most awful situations people can come together and support one another—you can handle just about anything.

Things Only White People Get Away With

- Being late
- Not paying taxes
- Not seasoning food
- Yelling at the cops
- Putting their kids on a leash
- Posting forty-eight photos of the avocado toast they had for breakfast
- "Forgetting" to pay the rent check on the first
- Putting their dogs in strollers
- Adding raisins to potato salad

CHAPTER 9

TROUBLE IN PARADISE: WHEN THE GOOD LIFE FEELS ALL WRONG

The first thing I noticed when I stepped into Mrs. Peters's tidy stucco house were the photographs. It was hard not to. They took up almost the entire far wall of the living room and were carefully arranged in a giant heart formation.

"I knew you'd like my display," Mrs. Peters said, gesturing toward the wall of photos, a tribute to her son, Lavar, who also happened to be my first serious boyfriend. "My baby boy has always been so very handsome," she added. "Girl, you got yourself a good man."

"Yes, Mrs. Peters," I said. "I sure do."

Lavar and I had met in our senior year at Prairie View. At the time, I was the head of the Pan-Hellenic Council, the organization that coordinated all Greek life on campus. I'd called a council meeting of fraternity and sorority reps to discuss our upcoming step show. The meeting was already in full swing when Lavar, who was repping Phi Beta Sigma, strolled in.

"You're late," I said.

He glanced around: "You talking to me?"

"You see anyone else walking in fifteen minutes late?"

Lavar shot me a flirtatious smile. "If I'd known you were chairing this meeting," he said, "I would have been here early." We started dating the very next week.

Lavar was a business major with big plans; at Prairie View we called guys like Lavar "go-getters."

"The goal is upper management," he told me one day as we walked to the library. "I'm talking corner office, six-figure salary, a good woman, and a couple of kids. It's the American dream and I'm gonna get it. Sounds good, right?"

"Yeah, Lavar," I said. "It sounds perfect."

I appreciated that Lavar had his eyes on the prize. But what I really liked was that his plans for the good life also included me. He said I was "wifey material" and that I was the perfect package of a "good mind" and "baby-making lips." The way he talked about our future together made us sound like the next black power couple, like Cliff and Claire Huxtable. It was the kind of life that most girls from Brewster-Douglass Projects only dreamed about. There was only one hitch: before we settled down, I wanted to start my career.

Prairie View was known for its excellent engineering program. By the time I was in senior year, recruiters from companies all over the country looking for entry-level engineers were flying me out for interviews. Back then, there were very few women or minorities working in electrical engineering, which is what I was majoring in. For companies looking to diversify, I was a great candidate. They could check off two diversity boxes and call it a day.

I met with almost a dozen HR people—at companies in Arkansas, South Carolina, Indiana, and California—who showed me around their offices and introduced me to the staff.

"I'm really excited about this opportunity," I told one re-cruiter. Then I said the same thing to a dozen more. Every place I went looked pretty much the same. The manager would be some white guy in pleated khakis, overseeing a staff so white that they looked like the audience at a Garth Brooks concert, working in an office filled with row upon row of gray cubicles. All the pale colors hurt my eyes.

I guess the managers wanted to add some color to the scenery because I received eight different job offers before I'd even graduated. In the end, it was Redd Foxx who helped me decide which one to take. I'd grown up on a steady diet of *Sanford and Son* reruns. Fred Sanford was constantly making fun of a place called El Segundo, a small town near LAX airport. (In one episode, he said his cheap Ripple fortified wine came from "the vineyards of El Segundo." Another time, Fred told his son Lamont that his Days in Paris cologne smelled "more like Nights in El Segundo.") When I learned that one of my job offers was to work as an engineer for Xerox out of their offices in El Segundo, I knew my decision had been made. How could I turn down a job in a city that was a constant punch line in one of my favorite shows?

"Everything is coming together real good," Lavar said when I told him. He'd already accepted a job offer at a soft drink company based in Southern California. It was his idea that the two of us move out to Cali together and stay at his mama's place while we saved up money to get a place of our own. "We can begin our lives together right now," he said. "Just like I planned."

That summer, I was full of hope and excitement. I had a college degree, a good man, a free place to live, and, most important, a job with dental benefits. I was on the road to happily ever after. What I didn't know was that sometimes all that happiness can be hard to take.

❧

Lavar's mama lived on a quiet street in Compton, in a one-story home that she welcomed me into with open arms. "It's so nice to have you, Loni," she said, leading me into the back bedroom that Lavar and I were to share. "Go on and make yourself right at home."

Mrs. Peters had been widowed for almost a decade, but it looked to me like she'd taken all the surplus affection left over when her husband died and transferred it to her sons. Lavar had an older brother who lived in Chicago, but Lavar was her "baby," her "little man." She doted on him with a love I'd never seen before.

There was the tribute wall—which Mrs. Peters diligently dusted every Sunday morning, right after she washed, folded, and pressed Lavar's laundry—and the neck massages she gave her "little man" every evening while he watched TV. But weekday mornings were when Mrs. Peters really went to town. She'd pop out of bed before the sun came up and sprint to the kitchen to get Lavar's hot breakfast together so her baby could start his day right. If it was up to me, I would have poured Lavar a mug of Cheerios and told him to eat it in the car on his way to work. But Mrs. Peters wouldn't dream of cold cereal for her prince. She served him grits and sausages or pancakes and scrambled eggs. If she could have, Mrs. Peters would have hatched those eggs herself.

I knew my mama did me wrong when she kicked me out of the house at seventeen. But seeing the way Mrs. Peters catered to her son made me wonder if there was a whole other level of parenting that I didn't know anything about. But Mrs. Peters set me straight. This wasn't about her being a good mama, she said, it was simply the way "a lady takes care of a man."

One Sunday, she pulled me into the kitchen. "You know how to cook, Loni?" she asked. I paused, like maybe this was a trick question. I thought back to the days I'd spent fending for myself in Mama's kitchen. I was a wiz at frying up Spam, and I could make a decent mac and cheese from a box. But I wouldn't call myself a chef. Especially not compared to Mrs. Peters, who looked like she was gunning for the role of black Martha Stewart.

"It's not my best talent," I told her.

"Well, if you're going to be with my boy, you better learn," she said with a smile. "He ain't gonna marry you if you don't feed him right." Mrs. Peters handed me an apron. Wife Training Boot Camp was officially in session.

Every Sunday afternoon, Mrs. Peters did her best to teach me how to cook. We made pot roast, baked chicken, beef stew, and collard greens. Nothing came out of a box and everything took hours and hours of cutting, chopping, and something I'd never heard of before called "basting." While we cooked, Mrs. Peters prattled on about Lavar. "He likes starch in his collars," she said one day, which confused the hell out of me because I thought "starch" was a kind of food. "You might want to write this down," she added, handing me a pen.

I tried my best with Mrs. Peters, nodding and smiling and taking notes. But it turns out I'm not a natural in the kitchen.

Things I Would Rather Do on a Sunday Than Spend the Day Cooking

- Have my tonsils removed
- Watch Schindler's List
- Get a Brazilian
- Look for my real father
- Listen to JoJo the Wino tell me his life story
- Bail my cousin Skillet out of jail
- Try to recover my Myspace account
- Watch someone else cook

One time, I accidentally left a plastic spatula in with the tuna casserole and baked it at 350 degrees for an hour. Another time, when I tried to serve a beef stew to Mrs. Peters and Lavar, they shook their heads no and said it didn't smell right. I gave it to the neighbor's pet poodle instead. Poor little guy. We gave him a nice burial in the yard though.

One Sunday afternoon, while Mrs. Peters and I were in the kitchen making cheese soufflé—which, as far as I can tell, is just mac and cheese without the mac—Mrs. Peters sat me down. "I've got something for you," she said. She told me to close my eyes. When I opened them again, there was a three-ring binder on the table in front of me. On the cover, in thick black marker, Mrs. Peters had written "Baby Boy's Favorite Foods."

"These are my best recipes," she said proudly, tapping the book. "I wrote them all out for you." Poor Mrs. Peters. It was like she had never heard of the "prepared food" section at the grocery store.

I opened my mouth to tell her about this great invention called a microwave. But before I could say a word, she reached down under her chair and pulled out a second, thicker binder. This one was called "House Cleaning." I noticed she'd made separate tabs for each room in the house.

"Now, this one," she announced, pulling out yet another binder, "I made especially for you, Loni."

I glanced at the cover: "Personal care."

"What is this?" I asked.

"It's about your...," Mrs. Peters waved her hand up and down, gesturing toward my body, "upkeep."

Upkeep? I looked down at my outfit. I was dressed in my casual home attire: a faded, oversized Prairie View hoodie, a pair of cutoff gym shorts, a head scarf, and no bra. I spent five days a week at my new engineering job at Xerox dressed in stockings and sensible pumps, and these were my comfy clothes. It hadn't ever occurred to me that I needed to look nice at home too.

"Go ahead," she said, pushing the binder toward me. "Take a look." Like the others, this book was divided into sections by brightly colored tabs. I flipped open to a page called "Bedtime Beauty." In her careful penmanship, Mrs. Peters had written out a nighttime beauty regimen that included applying long fake eyelashes right before bed. Noticing my look of confusion, she patted me gently on my arm. "It's okay," she said. "I know you got them big man-sized hands. You can start off with mascara."

"But why would I even wear makeup when I'm sleeping?"

"Oh, honey," she replied with a laugh. "It's not for *you*. It's in case Lavar wakes up in the middle of the night. You want to look your very best. When Lavar's daddy was alive—God rest his soul—I used to wear a full face and a Diahann Carroll wig to bed." Mrs. Peters paused and a slow smile crept across her face. "I had to fasten on that wig *real* good, too. I used an entire box of hairpins every night. Mr. Peters was a very passionate lover.

"Trust me," she added, again waving her hands in my direction, "you don't want to go to bed looking like a big ole mess. Listen up, chile, there is always some heifer waiting in the wings ready to snatch up a fine hardworking man like my Lavar. It's your job to keep your man happy at home."

My job? I already had a job.

"Another thing you might want to think about," Mrs. Peters continued, "is staying trim. I was a tight size eight when I got married. There's nothing attractive about a woman who lets herself go—"

I'd heard enough. I couldn't take any more self-improvement advice. "Thank you," I said abruptly, pushing myself away from the table and collecting my binders. "Thank you for your, uh, concern." Before Mrs. Peters could say another word, I hurried to the bedroom I shared with Lavar and closed the door behind me.

Mrs. Peters had me feeling like I'd failed a test I didn't even know I'd signed up for. It was obvious she expected me to master the art of cooking and cleaning and applying nighttime makeup. But I had no idea how to do any of those things. And until I moved in with her, I didn't know I had to.

I grew up in a home where nine-year-old kids were expected

to fend for themselves; it didn't occur to me that a grown man would need this much care and attention. It would be one thing if I didn't have a job. But I was already busting my ass eight hours a day at Xerox. There was no way I could come home and do a second shift.

I lay down on the bed and closed my eyes, overcome with fatigue. When I opened them again, the sun was streaming in through the bedroom window and Lavar was already dressed and gone for the day. I pulled on my stockings and my sensible shoes and headed out to work, too.

⌒

I used to think that working in corporate America—at a desk job with dental benefits and paid vacation—would be a breeze. Especially compared to busting my ass on the General Motors assembly line. But working at Xerox was an adjustment, for sure.

My job was to build the circuit boards that went inside copier machines. But it wasn't the work that got me stressed. I liked problem solving and figuring out how to make things go. I even liked working in a little cubicle. At Xerox, we got to decorate our work areas anyway we liked. Carol, whose cubicle was around the corner from mine, covered her walls in pictures of her family members, who, frankly, were not very photogenic. Imagine getting up to go to the ladies' room, turning a corner, and—*bam!*—there's a picture of Freddy Krueger staring right back at you.

I decided to go in a different direction and make my cubicle a treat for the whole staff. On one side, I put up a picture of my fantasy family, including my dream mama, Diana Ross, and my future husband, Tito Jackson. I also hung up a glossy eight-by-ten picture of the fine-as-hell Babyface Edmunds, the guy I was going to cheat on Tito with. The other side of my cubicle was for uplift and inspiration. I had a photo of my idol, Oprah Winfrey, and an inspiring quote from Maya Angelou: "Success is liking yourself, liking what you do and liking how you do it."

But I'm no dummy. I knew all my photos of black people might get my coworkers thinking I was planning some kind of uprising, so I also put up a poster of a little kitten doing a pull-up, with the caption "Hang in There!" Everybody knows white people love cats.

My cubicle was definitely the most festive in the office. It was also the most practical. In my bottom right-hand drawer, I kept a George Foreman grill. All the other folks on my floor brought cold sandwiches to work. But I enjoyed a nice hot meal in the middle of the day. When I saw George Foreman hawking his grill on TV late one night, I carefully reread my employee handbook and found there was no rule expressly forbidding any staff member from cooking up a beef patty or a chicken thigh at their desk. Thanks to that grill, and my fully stocked condiments shelf, I enjoyed the hell outta my lunch hour. It was the rest of corporate America that took some getting used to.

For one thing, I didn't realize that the minute a black woman walks into an office full of white people that all those coworkers would immediately start trying to connect with a sister by talking about whatever facts they happen to know about black folks.

Bob, my manager, was a big comedy fan. One day, he came

Ten Things You Should Never Say to the One Black Person in Your Office

- "Can I touch your hair?"
- "Man, this boss is a real slave driver, huh?"
- "I hope you don't expect to have Martin Luther King Day off..."
- "Our housekeeper LaKeisha is like family to us."
- "So, why can't I say the N-word?"
- Anything that starts with "You people..."
- "Do you know Snoop Dogg?"
- "I have lots of black friends."
- "I don't understand why Black History Month gets a WHOLE month."
- "Hey, Chocolate Thunder!"

up beside me with a big grin and asked, "Why don't white people leave when there's a ghost in the house?" I was about to say, "White privilege?" when I realized that Bob was repeating a joke from Eddie Murphy's *Delirious*. "That guy cracks me up," said Bob. To my horror, he started doing an Eddie Murphy impression, right there in the employee break room. "I had a mother who would throw a shoe at you at the drop of a dime...," Bob said in his best high-pitched Murphy voice.

Jim, from accounting, kept telling me about a safari he and

his wife went on during their honeymoon, in Kenya—which he referred to as "the Motherland."

"Dude," I finally said, "aren't you from Wisconsin?"

One day, Dave, who sat in the cubicle next to me, flipped open his wallet to show me a picture of a young black child dressed in shorts and a T-shirt. "That's my neighbor's kid," he said proudly, "he's adopted."

"He's real cute," I said, wondering if Dave's neighbors knew he had their child's picture in his wallet.

"Yeah, my neighbors are good people," he added. "They also have a dog they rescued from the pound."

I know my coworkers didn't mean to offend me. But sometimes it felt like we were from different planets. They were always touching my hair and asking me to explain rap lyrics to them. I know these aren't the worst things that can happen at work. It's not like Bob wore blackface to the Halloween staff party—or Jim said his plans for the weekend included checking out a Klan rally. But day in and day out I found myself having to answer the most stupid questions and explain the most basic facts. Like, "My hair did not grow overnight, Carol, it's a wig." And, "No, Jim, I don't know Esther Rolle." And, "Bob you can't say the N-word even if you do it in an Eddie Murphy voice."

When I was at Prairie View, I used to imagine that when I finally got an office job I'd love going to work. I thought the whole point of getting a college education was so I wouldn't have to come home every day feeling angry, like my mama did. But dealing with folks who had never worked with a black person before was hella exhausting. I'd been hired to be an engineer, but some days I felt like I had a second job teaching these folks remedial African American studies. I started making up excuses to go to the bathroom just so I could be alone (thank you, irritable bowel syndrome). I'd take my computer with me and stay in there all afternoon, enjoying the peace and quiet, and counting down the minutes until I could go home.

∼

After six months of living in his mama's house, Lavar and I had finally saved up enough money to move into our own apartment. While I appreciated everything Mrs. Peters had done for us, I was ready to go. I was tired of her giving me cooking lessons for food I would never make and sick of her remarks about my weight and my casual wear. I knew enough not to complain to Lavar about his mother. A mana's boy will always take his mother's side in a dispute, no matter how wrong she is. Instead, I bit my tongue and waited until the day he and I could get up out of that place and make a home of our own. *Hallelujah,* I thought as Lavar and I pulled out of his mama's driveway, *free at last.*

I looked over at Lavar and raised my eyebrows. "It's about to be on and poppin'," I said, trying to sound sexy. "Now you got me all to yourself."

I imagined the two of us doing all kinds of fun couple activities, like spending lazy Sunday afternoons napping on the sofa or enjoying romantic candlelit dinners of take-out Taco Bell. I thought for sure we'd kick off our life out of his mama's house by having some of that steamy-hot porno-type sex on the kitchen counter. Kitchen sex is why God gave twenty-year-olds strong backs and good knees. I was looking forward to having nonstop grown-ass fun. But I learned pretty quick that Lavar had other plans.

We'd been in our new place less than a week when Lavar woke me up with a tap on my shoulder. "Get up," he said.

I cracked open one eye and looked up at him. "You want some kitchen sex?" I asked. "Or is there a fire? Because I know you're not waking me up at the crack of dawn without a good reason."

"First of all," he said, "it's noon. And second, you have a ton of shit to do." He handed me a piece of paper with a carefully typed to-do list of forty-seven things I was supposed to accomplish that day, including "straighten the living room" and "clean out the fridge." I read the list and immediately burst out laughing.

"That's hilarious!" I said. "You know I love a man with a sense of humor." Then I turned over to resume my nap.

"I'm not joking," Lavar said coldly. And thus began what I like to think of as Lavar's multipart lecture series: "What Loni needs to do to make this relationship work."

"This is supposed to be a partnership," he explained. "I am the man. That means I provide and protect. As the woman, it's your responsibility to take care of the home. If I don't see that you can take care of the basics, how can I trust you with raising my children? This is a partnership," he said again. "You need to do your part." Without waiting for me to respond, Lavar walked out of the room and left the apartment, slamming the front door behind him.

I was stunned. All this time, I'd been looking forward to getting out from under Lavar's mama so we could build a relationship by our own set of rules. But it turned out Lavar's idea of coupling up was exactly like his mother's. He expected me to be a certain kind of woman—someone who would keep the house in order, support him in his endeavors, and wear mascara to bed. That was our first fight. Pretty soon, we were arguing every day.

Lavar didn't appreciate my weekend nap schedule, which he called "indulgent." He complained about the way I did the laundry, which was on the classic when-I-run-out-of-clean-drawers timetable. And when I tried to make him something to eat, he had the audacity to criticize the results. So what if I accidentally cooked a chicken without first removing the feathers? And who *hasn't* made a grilled cheese sandwich without setting their kitchen curtains on fire? No matter how I tried, nothing I did was ever good enough.

Unhappiness doesn't hit you all at once. It's more like the slow seep of an overflowing toilet. You don't realize you have a problem until you see water pouring out from under the bathroom door. During this period of my life—juggling work, a relationship, and all the expectations placed on me—I felt like I was drowning. At Xerox I felt like an outsider among coworkers; at home with Lavar, I felt even more alone. *Is this all there is to life,* I wondered, *serving a man and explaining black history to white people?* I had left Prairie View full of hope and excited for my brand-new life; now I just felt trapped.

I was so miserable that when I finished work at Xerox I started taking the long way home. And by "long way home" I mean instead of driving east, toward Compton, I'd turn my car and head in the other direction. Sometimes, I'd drive for hours.

The great thing about LA is there are all kinds of places where you can get away from it all. You can hike in Runyon Canyon or bird-watch in Griffith Park. You can head out to the Pacific Coast Highway and watch the sun go down at the beach. I could have gone any of those places to unwind. But I'm from Detroit. We don't do hills, and we don't like the sand. Instead, I took my ass north, to the bright lights of West Hollywood. I didn't need nature to feel better—what I needed was some laughs.

Hollywood's famed Sunset Strip, between Doheny and Fairfax, is home to two of the greatest comedy clubs in the world, the Laugh Factory and the Comedy Store, which is exactly where I found myself late one Tuesday night. Everybody who is anybody has performed at the Comedy Store: Robin Williams, David Letterman, Roseanne Barr, Eddie Murphy. But that night there was no big-name headliner. Instead, there was a string of comics I'd never heard of. One guy did a bit about playing sports with his son, another told jokes about trying to clean his apartment. The third guy talked about a message his mother left on his answering machine.

Only one woman performed. She was tall and blond and looked to be in her late thirties. She talked about her husband, her three children, her angry mother-in-law, and a faulty birth-control product she'd bought called a diaphragm. "My first kid should sue the manufacturer," she said, with a smirk. "He was supposed to be an only child."

I'd never heard of a diaphragm and didn't relate to any of her stories, but I loved the way the room erupted in laughter with every joke she told. The woman looked out at the audience and beamed. She was radiating a kind of happiness that I realized I hadn't felt in months. Not since I was in college. Not since I was up onstage at the Student Center at Prairie View doing my one-woman show.

When we were still at school, Lavar had painted me a picture of the "perfect" life we'd have together, striving for middle management, marriage, and a two-car garage. But that was *his* fantasy, not mine. Sitting in the back of that dark club watching the comic with the spotlight shining down on her and hearing laughter all around, I had an epiphany that would change everything. In that moment, staring up at the stage, I realized what I wanted more than anything was a life filled with the thrill of making other people laugh.

When I got home that night, I started packing up my stuff. "I'm moving out," I told Lavar. "I'm breaking up with you and your mama." I guess he was tired of my ass, too, because for the first time since we'd moved in together, he didn't try to argue.

The very next week, I moved into my own apartment. I had come to California to start a brand-new life. This time I was going to do it right.

Ten Signs Your Relationship Is in Trouble

- He won't leave his wife.
- He still lives in his mama's basement.
- You can't stand the way he blinks.
- You set up an online dating profile to help him find someone new.
- You ask his mama to talk bad about you.
- He hasn't been home in three days and you didn't notice.
- You get a second job just to be out of the house.
- You call him another guy's name in bed, but he doesn't notice because he's in the other room jerking off.
- You go on a farting spree just to get out of having sex.
- You give him all your passwords so he can see you're cheating on him.

CHAPTER 10

"WHERE'S THE CRACK?" HOW I LEARNED I GOTTA BE ME

Claire La Monroe pushed her gray hair out of her eyes. "Loni," she said, "you're killing me." Her words hit me like a punch to the belly.

Since breaking up with Lavar, I'd been on a mission to kick-start my new life. The first thing I did was enroll in Claire La Monroe's "So You Want to Do Stand-Up?" comedy class, which I'd learned about from a flyer hanging on a bulletin board near a restroom at a comedy club. According to Claire's website, she was a "world-renowned" teacher of "comedy arts." So, I'd put everything I had into coming up with two minutes of material to perform in her introduction-to-comedy workshop. But now she was telling me, in front of the entire class, that my comedy wasn't any good.

"Can I try again?" I asked.

"No," Claire answered, motioning me off the small stage. "Give someone else a turn. You can try again next week." I was so embarrassed I could barely look at the other students as I made my way back to my seat.

I'd paid $300 for six weeks of lessons, which Claire taught every Tuesday night out of a small rehearsal space in Burbank. Despite the humiliation of having Claire La Monroe tell me I wasn't funny, I was still convinced her comedy class was money well spent. What really got me excited was that for the last class, Claire put on a showcase at a local comedy club where her students could perform in front of a live audience. To me, the chance to perform at a Hollywood comedy club was worth the money. All I wanted was to get onstage.

I wasn't the only one with a dream. My classmate Juan Carlos worked at Best Buy during the day but said he'd wanted to do comedy ever since he saw *Raw*. "I'm gonna be the Spanish Eddie Murphy," he said. Annabelle was an English major at UCLA; she insisted she'd always been the "class clown," which I found hard to believe because all Annabelle did was complain about men. Claire called this Annabelle's "shtick." Rudy was a middle-aged, stick-thin, balding manager at an Albertsons grocery store where, he claimed, everyone said he was hilarious. "I have *a lot* of material," he kept saying. "Don't even get me started. My ex-wife is fucking insane. *In-fucking-sane*. I got material out the wazoo."

I was nervous on the first day of class, but as soon as I met my classmates I relaxed. For one thing, I was sure there was no way these weirdos were funnier than me. For another, I was the only one in Claire's class with any experience in live entertainment. I had killed at the highly competitive Brewster-Douglass Junior Talent Show when I was nine, and I got some of the best laughs the Prairie View Student Center had ever seen with my one-woman Wanda Winfrey talk show. I even had some stand-up under my belt. While I was in college, I used to do open mic contests at a local bar, where the bar manager offered fifty dollars' prize money to the performer who got the most laughs.

I'd get up on the little stage at the back of the bar, talk about college life and Amber's latest shenanigans, and win that prize money every time. Compared to the newbies in Claire's comedy class, I was practically a professional. Apparently, Claire didn't agree.

The first time I performed in front of her, I had given her what I thought was a solid joke about take-your-kids-to-work day: "Who the hell came up with this idea? People go to work to *leave* their kids." When I had tried out the joke the day before in the break room at Xerox, Bob had laughed so hard his Diet Dr Pepper came out his nose. But comedy expert Clair La Monroe didn't even crack a smile.

After she waved me off the stage, she turned back to give me another note. "The problem with your material," she said, "is that it just doesn't feel *authentic*."

Authentic. There was that word again. Claire La Monroe said it a lot.

❧

Claire liked to start every comedy class with a thirty-minute lecture during which she'd share her tips for success. Sometimes her tips made sense, like when she said, "Write what you know." I took that to mean don't try to fake the funk and write jokes about shit you know nothing about. I didn't want to hear some middle-age white guy making jokes about what it means to be a twenty-something black woman. And I was sure nobody wanted to hear me try to do comedy about raising four kids in the suburbs. But other times, Claire's instructions left me scratching my head, like when she said, "Be authentic" and "Find your voice." How was I supposed to find something that wasn't lost? After a few classes, I began to think that maybe there were lessons I needed to learn that Claire couldn't teach.

The weekend after Claire told me I sucked, I took a road trip to the Museum of Television and Radio, in Beverly Hills, to study up. I slid into a booth, put on some headphones, and watched hours of TV appearances by some of the best comedians in the world, from Richard Pryor to Joan Rivers. Sometimes I turned off the sound and observed how comedians would cue the audience that they were getting ready to tell a joke with a slightly raised eyebrow or a wide-open grin. I watched performances by comics my mama used to play on her little record player when her friends came over on Friday nights, like Bill Cosby, Rodney Dangerfield, and Redd Foxx. And I watched a lot of women comics, like Roseanne Barr, Rosie O'Donnell, and Ellen DeGeneres, who I especially loved. She seemed so warm and goofy, like the kind of friend who could make going to the gynecologist fun.

One comic in particular caught my attention. Moms Mabley was one of the first female stand-ups in the country, and she was black. Moms had a really hard life—her father, a firefighter, was killed in an explosion when she was eleven, and her mother was hit by a truck and killed on Christmas Day. As a child, she was raped twice, once at age eleven and again two years later by a white sheriff; both times she'd become pregnant and both times those children were given away—but despite her hardships, she made a successful career in comedy. Instead of talking about her troubles, Moms made people crack up talking about how old her husband was and how much she lusted after young men. Not only was Moms Mabley the first female comedian to perform at the Apollo, she also recorded numerous comedy albums and even starred in the feature film *Amazing Grace*. At the height of her career, she was earning $10,000 a week just for making people laugh.

I wasn't exactly sure what Claire meant by finding my voice, but I did come to understand that there are a lot of different ways to be funny. Richard Pryor forced his audience to confront uncomfortable truths, like racism; Jerry Seinfeld specialized in making funny observations about everyday life; and Joan Rivers's best jokes involved putting herself down.

I wondered about the kind of comic I wanted to be. I knew I wasn't "raw" or "edgy," and I didn't want to shock or offend. I wanted my comedy to be a reflection of myself, warm and easygoing. I wanted to be the kind of performer who you'd see onstage and think, "I'd like to invite her over for a fun night of drinking cocktails and taking pics for my Tinder profile." Most of all, I wanted to make jokes about the world I saw around me, like the crazy shit that happened at work every day. Because there is nothing funnier than cubicle life.

⌒

The next Tuesday when Claire called on me to do my set, I got up and tried my material again. "Have you ever noticed how people who work in offices decorate their cubicles...," I began.

"Wait, wait, stop right there," Claire said, putting her hands up like a traffic cop. "What's going on?"

I looked around wondering who she was talking to.

"You, Loni," she said. "I'm talking to you. What are you doing right now?"

This felt like a trick question: "I'm doing comedy?"

"No, no, no, no, no. What are you doing right *now?* Onstage. What are you talking about? Is this supposed to be some kind of Seinfeld bit?"

"No . . . Wait . . . *What?*"

"It looks like you're doing an observational bit about the mundanity of office life. You know, like 'What's the deal with cubicles?'" Claire said in a pretty good Seinfeld. "But I think what an audience wants from you is more personal. More of you speaking from your own experience."

"This is my experience," I said. "I work in an office."

"No, no, no, no," she continued. "I mean, give them something more *unique* and *authentic.* Like, where did you grow up?"

"Detroit."

"Okay, that's good. Give me more of that. What kind of neighborhood was it?"

"Uh, the hood?"

"Love that, tell me more."

"I grew up in the projects."

"Fantastic!"

"But I work in an office now. I'm an engineer . . ."

"Loni, everybody works in an office. We want your unique experience. In the hood."

I just stared at her.

"Were there drug dealers?" she continued. "Drive-bys? Give me some of that gritty hardscrabble life you lived."

I wanted to tell Claire that I didn't know anything about selling drugs or doing drive-bys. I wanted to tell her I played the French horn. But she was on a roll and I couldn't get a word in edgewise.

"The grit, the grime, the carnage...Who were your friends growing up in the projects?"

"I had a friend named Peaches."

"'Peaches,' that sounds funny!" she said, brightening up.

"She got shot."

"Oh."

"She died."

"Okay, that's not funny,—forget Peaches....What else? Do you have any stories about crack? Dealing crack, maybe? Smoking crack? Like maybe you *dabbled* in the crack?" I stared at her blankly. "Okay," she said. "Let's try this again. Show me what you got."

I cleared my throat and gave it another shot. "So, I work at Xerox," I said, my voice trembling with nerves, "and I was in my cubicle..."

Claire just shook her head. I didn't want to mess up in front of my whole class again. I had to think fast and save my joke. "So, I reached under my desk," I continued, "and, um...I pulled out some crack."

❡

Comedy is not an easy industry to break into for anybody, but back in the day, it was especially difficult for women and black folks to get a break. If you looked back at the roster of comics who got to play the biggest clubs before the 2000s, you'd see dozens of male performers for every woman who got a gig. People thought nobody wanted to see women telling jokes onstage. In the 1970s, the owner of the Comedy Store, Mitzi Shore, even opened a smaller room within the club, called the Belly Room, that was just for women. The Comedy Store's Main Room has five hundred seats; the Belly Room only seats seventy—it was like comedy purgatory.

Back then, all the important people who could make your career—agents, managers, and bookers for *The Tonight Show*—scouted for talent in the Main Room; nobody checked for talent in the Belly Room where the women performed. If you were black, the odds of getting an audience were even slimmer.

Huge stars like Redd Foxx and Richard Pryor, and later Eddie Murphy, got booked at the hottest comedy venues. But most club owners assumed that only black audiences would pay money to hear lesser-known black comics, and so they wouldn't book anyone without a marquee name. In response, comics and promoters got together and created spaces where black acts could perform. Sometimes, a promoter would book a specific night at a mainstream comedy club, call it something like "Hot Chocolate," and feature all black comics in the lineup. Other times, "black night" was held at little hole-in-the-wall bars. In the comedy world, these shows are known as the "Chitlin Circuit," named after the string of venues that allowed black musicians and entertainers to perform during the Jim Crow era, when they couldn't get booked anywhere else.

Folks think segregation is a thing of the past. But by the 1990s, just before I was breaking into comedy, it was still hard for black comics to get booked at mainstream clubs. Then, something happened that changed the game completely. On

Friday nights at midnight, HBO started airing a groundbreaking new comedy show featuring nothing but black stand-ups. *Def Comedy Jam* exploded into living rooms all over America. Comedy would never be the same.

Def Comedy Jam was the most earth-shattering thing to happen to comedy since the invention of the laugh track. Created by Russell Simmons, the founder of legendary hip-hop record label Def Jam, the program showcased black comics who had the same raw energy as the hottest nineties rappers. It was as if 2 Live Crew, Dr. Dre, and Trina did stand-up.

A lot of these comics were really good. Some of them, like Sommore, Earthquake, Sheryl Underwood, and Adele Givens, were amazing. They'd been honing their craft on the Chitlin Circuit for years, at places like Chocolate Sundaes in Los Angeles and the Peppermint Lounge in Newark, New Jersey. And black audiences do not mess around. If you aren't funny, they will boo your ass offstage, or worse. I've seen people throw car keys and empty glasses at comics who weren't making them laugh. If you don't have a tight set, you're pretty much risking your life when you get onstage at a black club. The audience will knock your block off if you can't tell a joke. *Def Jam* comics had trained in comedy war zones, and they brought a kind of energy to TV a lot of white folks had never seen before.

Def Comedy Jam was a massive hit and made a whole lot of black comics famous. But as much as the show put comics like Martin Lawrence, Chris Tucker, and Bernie Mac on the map, there was also a downside. Because there is *always* a downside.

Def Comedy Jam quickly became synonymous with a very particular type of humor—profanity-filled, and focused on a few very specific topics, namely, sex, more sex, the difference between black and white people, oral sex, food you get in the hood, baby mamas and chicken heads, and sex. A lot of the comics liked to act out fornication, humping the stool in every possible position. They left DNA samples all over that stage. The problem isn't that the material wasn't funny. It's that it created an expectation that the only way for a black comic to be successful was for him or her to do *Def Jam*–type jokes, filled with all kinds of muthafucka this and muthafucka that.

I think when Claire saw me—a curvaceous black woman from the projects—all she thought was *Def Jam,* and it prevented her from actually *seeing* me.

⌒

Week after week, Claire directed me to "keep it real," by which she meant "talk about life in the hood." By the second-to-last class, I had a solid five-minute set filled with F bombs and "muthafuckas," and I even did a little stool fornication. ("This is how we do it in the projects!" I said, humping the stool. Then I jumped up and hid behind it. "We got so many drive-bys sometimes you have to use your sex partner as a human shield.")

"Loni," Claire said, "this is so raw. I love it!"

I glanced around at the other students. Anabelle was examining her cuticles. Juan Carlos had a look on his face like a white guy just tried to teach him Spanish. After class, he approached me in the parking lot. "I'm no expert," he said. "But my two cents? That shit about take-your-kids-to-work day and all that? That shit is mad funny. I work at Best Buy," he added. "So, I get the whole corporate America thing."

I thanked Juan Carlos for the compliment, told him I loved

his bit about his grandma's roosters, and got into my car more confused than ever.

Claire was happy because I'd taken her notes to "put some sassy black girl in it" and "represent" like a girl from the hood. But the truth was, even though Claire liked my jokes, to me they never felt right. As proud as I was of my roots in Brewster-Douglass, I didn't want to talk about my past like this. The hood, my mama, ketchup sandwiches, being poor, the crack epidemic—it was all part of a world I had worked hard to escape. I didn't think it was funny when I was living among crack dealers and cockroaches, and I didn't want to turn that life into jokes, now that I was out.

Besides, I didn't think I had to. If Seinfeld could make a career commenting on everyday stuff he noticed all around him, why couldn't I?

Our graduation showcase was scheduled for eight o'clock on a Tuesday night at a small comedy club in Santa Monica. The night of the show, I drove to the club with what felt like bats flying around my stomach. I was going to be performing in front of real comedy fans—not a bunch of little kids in a rec center or college kids at a hole-in-the-wall bar—and I had to make them laugh.

At the venue, Claire gathered the class together and had us choose numbers out of a paper bag to determine the order we'd go up onstage. I pulled an eight, the second-to-last spot on the showcase. When the lights went down, I stood at the back of the bar and watched my classmates perform. Anabelle was up first. For five straight minutes, she complained about dating—bad food, bad company, and bad dick. Then Juan Carlos went up. He got some good laughs talking about wearing slippers with socks. Then it was my turn.

On my way to the stage, I passed Juan Carlos who grabbed me by the arm. "Do you, girl," he whispered in my ear. "Fuck Claire, she don't know your life. That cubicle shit was dope." His words stopped me dead in my tracks.

Sometimes people are put in your life to tell you exactly what you need to hear—like when a man in a crisp white dress shirt approaches you on a General Motors assembly line and suggests you go to college. This was one of those times. I'd been studying with Claire for six weeks and each week she said "Be authentic" and "Find your voice." But I didn't really get it until Juan Carlos whispered in my ear. If I wanted to be authentic and real, I had to do what felt right to me.

I stepped onstage with the spotlight shining bright in my face and my heart beating through my chest. I tried to block out everyone—Claire, the audience, my classmates—and speak my truth. "My name is Loni Love," I said, looking out at the crowd. A hundred faces peered back at me expectantly. This was my moment to choose my truth over the reality someone else assumed for me. This was the fork in the comedy road.

"I'm an engineer," I began, "and I work in a building with rows and rows of cubicles. Everybody tries to outdo everyone else decorating their cubicles. My coworker Carol has pictures of her ugly-ass family members all up in her cubicle. Nobody wants to see that! It's just rude. Now, I try to be nice to my coworkers. In my cubicle, I have my computer, and a little radio. You know what else I have under my desk?" I paused, looked around the room, and smiled. "I got me a George Foreman grill." For five minutes, I talked about office life cooking chicken things at my cubicle and teaching my white coworkers black history. When I finished my set, I got a standing O.

I learned an important lesson that night. Claire—the supposed comedy "expert"—didn't know shit about me or what I could do onstage. You know who does know what kind of comedy I do best? Me, that's who. And also, Juan Carlos. All Claire knew is what I looked like. For her, that was enough to decide who I should be.

Claire was the first industry expert to try to mold me to fit her expectations. But she sure as hell wasn't the last. Fighting other people's assumptions is a challenge I've had to face for most of my career. I'm hardly alone.

No matter who you are or where you go in this life, people are going to try to put you into a box. Once they put you there, they're going to try to convince you that it's the best place for you to be. But if they are wrong about you, you've got to stand up and let them know it. In comedy and in life, you can't expect people to give you permission to be yourself. You have to march onstage, claim your space, tell your story, and live your truth. If you don't do it, who the hell will?

Raw, Real, and Raunchy: Def Comedy Jam Sampler

- "I ain't got no man, but between Oprah and my gynecologist, I'm satisfied. I've learned to appreciate that pap smear, they come talking 'bout 'Once a year,' I'm like, 'Bullshit, I'll see you tomorrow.'" —Adele Givens
- "Two drinks might get your dick sucked, but one drink ain't gon' get you shit." —Sheryl Underwood
- "I'm forty years old. I'm at the point in my life where I do not want to make love, goddammit! I wanna fuck. I wanna fuck till I destroy some shit. I wanna fuck till the four walls come down. I want to fuck till a bird fly over and shit in my bed." —Simply Marvelous
- "I remember my first bikini wax...she pulled the paper back and I was like 'AHH, bitch, you don ripped off my coochie lips and everything, my uterus is on that fucking paper, bitch, how am I ever gonna get child support now, you ruined my life, bitch!'" —Tiffany Haddish
- "Last week somebody drank my cold, cold Pepsi. I had my whole family, grandma and

everybody, at gunpoint waiting for the first motherfucker to burp." —Brooklyn Mike

- "The Big Bad Wolf jumped out the bushes and said, 'Little Red Riding Hood, I'm gonna throw you down and fuck you to death.' Little Red Riding Hood said, 'No you ain't, you gon' eat me just like the book say.'" —Barbara Carlyle

- "Nobody don't give a fuck about OJ and all that punk-ass shit. Niggas just want to know: When is the next riot?" —Hope Flood

- "Every lady in the room clap if you'd suck a man dick for four million dollars. Now all y'all should be clapping. 'Cause I know some of y'all probably sucking dick for a Happy Meal." —Anthony Johnson

- "I'm in the bar cooling out, minding my own business. Just being cool, like I am. Woman come up to me: 'Mac, can I ask you a question?' I say, 'yeah.' She say, 'Does pussy taste like pumpkin pie?' Made me mad as hell. Don't ask me no damn question like that! I never had no pumpkin pie! —Bernie Mac

- "Everybody's a thief. The other day I robbed a store, came back out, and a nigga had stole my car." —Chris Tucker

CHAPTER 11

WHO YOU CALLING FAT?

In Los Angeles nobody is what they seem. The dog walker is actually an aspiring screenwriter; the girl waiting on you at the diner just wrapped her first feature film. LA is the land of dreamers, where everyone is hustling and striving and working on "their craft," convinced they are just one lucky break away from fame. After I killed at my graduation performance for Claire La Monroe's stand-up comedy class, I began to dream of stardom, too. I knew I had raw talent. All I needed was practice.

I was on a mission to get stage time wherever and whenever I could. That meant working the Chitlin Circuit in and around LA. Sometimes I'd wait hours just to do a five-minute set. On Monday nights, I'd hit up Michael Colyar's room at the Townhouse on Centinela Avenue. Tuesdays, I'd check out Larry La La's room at the back of Rosco's Chicken and Waffles. On Wednesdays, my friend Roz Browne ran a show at a small coffee shop on 48th and Crenshaw. Thursday nights, the place to be was Kat Williams's room at the Hollywood Park Casino. On Fridays, Ricky Harris did his thing at the Comedy Act

Theater. These were not moneymaking gigs. If I was lucky, I'd get paid "gas money," usually around twenty-five bucks. The Latin clubs out in East LA paid better; occasionally, I'd make as much as a hundred dollars a night. Sometimes, I wouldn't get paid at all.

But it was worth it. Getting stage time is the only way to hone your craft as a comedian. There is simply no other way to learn how to work a room. And if you want to learn how to survive a tough crowd, there's no better training than the Chitlin Circuit. Audiences in black rooms do not play.

Before I started doing stand-up, I figured the worst thing that could happen to a performer is you get booed off the stage. I learned pretty fast that getting booed is *not* the worst thing at all. At least when you get booed or the crowd throws napkins at the stage or tells you your mama's a bitch, you have something to work with. You can come back from being booed. In fact, the actual worst thing that can happen to a comedian is when you get up, tell a joke, and hear crickets. Silence from the audience will send any comic into a panic. It happened to me plenty of times when I was first starting out. I'd tell a joke about cubicle life and...nothing. Not even a chuckle. I'd be up onstage with sweat running down my back, scanning the room for any friendly face, trying to figure out how to get a laugh. It was humbling, but that's how I learned.

The first thing I figured out was how to make a connection with the crowd. I had to let the audience know who I was and where I was coming from. I started opening with a little self-deprecating humor. I'd wear mismatched socks and say, "Okay, I see you looking at my socks. I had to get dressed in the dark because my lights got cut off." That would always get a laugh.

Then, I might talk about my time at General Motors, like, "I used to work on the line at GM. I was supposed to start work at three in the morning. But I just left the club at two! My job was to put forty-five screws in the engine. I would put in two screws, and be like, 'Uh...it'll be a'ight.'" That would always get a laugh, too.

Sometimes, I'd get up and riff. Maybe I'd see something on the news—say, about the war in Iraq or the high price of avocados—and just start talking off the top of my head, trying to catch a joke. It's called "writing from the stage," and I've seen a lot of comics go down in flames trying to pull it off. But when you land on a riff that kills, there is no better feeling.

For two years, I spent a lot of nights driving around Southern California, going from one shitty club to another. I was putting in my time because I was sure one day it would all be worth it.

I had big plans for myself, secret dreams I didn't share with anyone. I had studied the career trajectories of comics who came before me and noticed that while male comics had, for decades, been able to transition from stand-up comedy to starring in movies and on TV, more recently, women like Roseanne and Ellen were getting those same kinds of deals. I figured if I put in the work and got in front of the right people, maybe one day I could be on TV, too.

I had a dream, but it's not like I was trying to give up my day job. I knew "gas money" doesn't pay the rent. Instead, I lived a double life. Monday to Friday, from nine to five, I worked at Xerox with Carol, Jim, and Bob; nights and weekends, I got onstage to make folks laugh. Sunday was my one day off to relax and do my chores. It was my "me time." I didn't do anything fancy, like take salsa lessons or go to brunch with my gay pals. I liked to keep it low-key. I'd wake up around two in the afternoon, read the paper, make myself some coffee, and then head out for an energizing speed walk around my local grocery store.

One thing about growing up in the hood is you appreciate the hell out of a decent supermarket. When I was running my grocery delivery service at Brewster-Douglass, I did all my food shopping at the corner store. The place was a dump. The fresh produce display never had more than three overripe bananas and four waxy red apples. And most of the canned goods and boxes of cereal were well past their expiration dates. In comparison, the Ralphs grocery store near the apartment I moved into after I broke up with Lavar was heaven on earth. It was brightly lit and spotlessly clean, with soothing Muzak renditions of Elton John hits playing over the loudspeaker. Sometimes, I'd be shopping, turn a corner, and—surprise!—there would be some friendly Ralphs employees giving away free samples of fifteen-dollar hummus spread on organic multigrain crackers. The only place I'd seen people hand out free food in Detroit was at the soup kitchen.

What I liked most about Ralphs was the size. The place was as big as a football field. That's why I always wore my sneakers. I figured if I kept up a good clip as I made my way up and down the aisles, I could count grocery shopping as a vigorous workout.

One Sunday afternoon while I was springing down the

cookie aisle on my weekly food shopping slash exercise sesh, I heard a small child call out: "She is *so* FAT!"

"Shhh...," I heard an adult voice say. "That's not nice." I turned my head to see who this kid was insulting. I expected to see a giant woman in one of those electric scooters. To my surprise, the aisle was empty except for me and a little boy in a striped T-shirt. He was riding in a shopping cart pushed by his mother, who was doing her best to avoid eye contact.

"Fat!" he repeated, pointing a finger right at me. "You're big *and* fat, like Shrek!"

I stared at him, speechless. No one in my life had ever called me fat before. And certainly not someone who wasn't even grown enough to wipe his own ass.

"I'm sorry," his mother said. "Ethan just blurts out whatever's on his mind..."

"Hmmmph," I replied, shooting Ethan a Brewster-Douglass side-eye that I hoped sent the message: "Say that again, and I WILL kick your tiny ass!" Then I power-walked my way out of the store.

∽

I've been a big girl all my life. But growing up, I was never what you'd call "fat." In the black community, where we appreciate women with curves, I was considered "thick" or "thic" or "big boned" ("big boned-ed" if you're country). I've been called "juicy," "bootylicious," and "booty-full." Once in a while, I'd get "well-fed" or "full-figured" or, my personal favorite, "sturdy." But "fat"? Hell to the muthafucking no.

As I made my way to the parking lot, still fuming, I thought for a second of turning around, finding that smart-ass kid, and giving him a piece of my mind. I imagined telling him he was rude, lazy, and, pretty damn short. But with those credentials, I figured he'd probably end up running a movie studio one day, and I might need him to give me a job. I was still mad when I got home. But I was also kind of curious. What was it that made that little smart-ass call me fat? I had to see for myself.

I went to my bedroom, slid out of my hoodie and my shorts, and stood in front of my full-length mirror. I turned around to get a clear view of what I looked like from behind. Then I bent over and did a little jiggle. For the record, I do not recommend doing this while sober. From the back, you can really see the full landscape of your body. It turns out I had all kinds of hills and valleys I didn't know existed. My curves had their own curves. It was like I was seeing myself for the first time.

I walked back to my living room with a pit in my stomach. How had I not noticed this before? I knew I had gained some weight since moving to LA—maybe twenty or thirty pounds, I figured. At the *most* sixty. Maybe sixty-five, but who's counting? I had started gaining while I was living with Lavar and his mother. The more they criticized me, the more I ate. I was protesting my mistreatment the way prisoners go on hunger strikes, only I was doing it in reverse. When I finally moved out, I didn't worry about taking off the weight. I was too busy living my life. Meanwhile, the pounds kept on creeping on.

What can I say? I like food. I don't mean that I'm a "foodie" who knows the names of the hottest new restaurants. I mean, I enjoy food like any red-blooded American: I like Taco Bell, KFC, and potato chips that come in a tube. I like all the hot, greasy comfort food that I missed out on as a child.

So what? I thought, settling on my sofa with a can of Pringles by my side. *Who cares if I put on a few pounds? It just means I'm more voluptuous and there ain't nothing wrong with that.* I was about to play Sir Mix-a-Lot's "Baby Got Back," aka the curvy girl's anthem, when my mind was suddenly filled with thoughts of something that had happened a few months earlier, a memory I'd been trying hard to push away.

I'd gone to an audition for a TV show that was in development at the now-defunct UPN network. The open casting, which was posted in *Backstage L.A.,* called for someone to play a "twenty-something professional black woman" as part of an ensemble cast in a network sitcom about single life in LA. As a twenty-something professional black woman living single in LA, I was perfect for the role. The only thing that would have made me a better fit for the part was if they'd included my shoe size.

When I arrived at the audition, I found the waiting room filled with black women of all shapes and sizes—just like real life. But when the pilot hit the air a few months later, on September 11, 2000, the cast didn't reflect the diverse group of women I'd seen at the casting at all. Instead, *Girlfriends* looked more like some TV exec's fantasy. Each woman was the size of a toothpick. How are you going to have a show about black women sister-friends, and every single woman is a size 2? Don't get me wrong, I know *Girlfriends,* which featured the brilliant Tracee Ellis Ross in her first prime-time starring role, is one of the best, and funniest, sitcoms of the early 2000s. At least, that's what I've been told. I was so disappointed I hadn't been cast that I would run to change the channel every time the show came on. For eight years, while *Girlfriends* was on the air, anytime Tracee Ellis Ross flashed across my screen I'd hit the living room floor, doing shoulder rolls like a Navy SEAL diving for the remote.

At first, I was convinced I didn't get cast in *Girlfriends* because I wasn't talented enough. But sitting on my sofa after the incident at the grocery store, a thought struck me for the very first time: Maybe the little brat in the cookie aisle understood more about the industry than I did. Maybe I didn't get the part because I didn't *look* the part. Maybe I didn't have a chance at TV because I was too damn fat.

If I were a white man, my weight wouldn't matter. Kevin James, Chris Farley, Norm from *Cheers,* Roseanne's husband, Lou Costello, Santa Claus...I could think of plenty of successful full-figured white guys. Even porn star Ron Jeremy, who is fat as fuck and *worked in the nude,* had an easier time getting ahead in show business than I did. That's what I call FWMP— fat white male privilege. In comparison, I could think of only *one* full-figured black woman with a starring role in a sitcom at the time: Mo'Nique, who played Nikki Parker on *The Parkers.* Only one sister with curves had a full-time TV gig. That's it. Those were not good odds at all.

Girlfriends wasn't the only audition that didn't go my way. I'd tried out for soap commercials and shampoo ads. I'd auditioned for roles as wives, girlfriends, and blind dates, but I didn't get any of those jobs, either. The only gig I managed to land was in a commercial for a fast-food chain. No one wanted to hire me as a woman. They only wanted to see me eat.

I couldn't believe I hadn't realized this before. I was a curvy cocoa-skinned black woman. If I was going to be successful in Hollywood, I was going to have to change.

I called it my "Year of Transformation" and it was going to be the ultimate glow-up. Like when the skinny, short, pimply kids get out of school for summer break, then come back in the fall new and improved and become instantly popular. Like, "Jonelle got some double DDs!" or "Harrison's a foot taller!" or "Dianne's acne cleared up!" In the movies, an extreme makeover is an express ticket to a better life.

The plan was, I'd take a year off and focus all my attention on dropping a smooth ninety-five pounds. Never mind that the last time I weighed that little I was in junior high school. If I was going to make it in LA, I needed an LA body. Once I was transformed, I'd come back on the scene, slimmed down and ready for pilot season.

In my imagination, there was a Halle Berry–sized woman trapped under all my curves. Loni "Halle Berry" Love did not get asked to do fried chicken commercials. No, Loni "Halle Berry" Love landed commercials for bubble bath and got cast in kissing scenes opposite Denzel. Loni "Halle Berry" Love was everything America wanted. All I had to do was set my inner Halle Berry free.

There was only one problem: I didn't know the first thing about losing weight. Growing up, the only thing my mama ever said about food was, "You better finish that." In my house, if you were lucky enough to have food on your plate, you damn well better eat it. I didn't know anything about a diet, so I figured I'd kick off my weight-loss transformation with a rigorous exercise program instead.

Finding a gym was easy enough. In Los Angeles, there are

gyms on every corner, right where McDonald's are supposed to be. I found a place not far from my apartment, signed up for a yearly membership, then headed to the mall to buy myself some workout gear.

I had never shopped for exercise clothes before, but I decided to treat myself to the very best because that's what Halle Berry would do. At the mall, I went straight to an upscale exercise wear store that shall remain nameless (but it just might rhyme with BooBoo Bemons). The minute I set foot in the door, I regretted my decision.

Just like the rest of Hollywood, this yoga pants emporium wasn't made for people like me. It was designed to cater to women who were already skinny, which makes people like me feel as though we don't belong. Things are different now. These days there are all kinds of talk about "body positivity," "fat acceptance," and "big girl beauty." You can find plus-size models in fashion magazines and full-figured mannequins in the windows of Nike stores. But back then, nobody was trying to call a full-figured woman "beautiful." In fact, I got the distinct impression the miniature-sized yoga-pants-wearing salespeople didn't want me in their store.

One of them came running toward me, her ponytail flapping behind her. "I'm here!" she called to her coworkers. "I've got this!" Gently, she took me by the elbow and ushered me toward the change rooms at the back of the store. "We don't keep the, uh, plus sizes on the floor," she explained in a whisper. "We keep them in the storeroom. Just wait here."

I stood in that dressing room, getting angrier by the minute. It felt like she was trying to keep me hidden from the other customers in the mall. *They should have hung a sign outside:*

Only skinny bitches allowed, I thought. I didn't even try on the cheetah-print capri workout leggings the manager finally brought me. I left the store and speed-walked my ass to Lane Bryant, where they appreciate sturdy customers like me. But as uncomfortable as I felt buying workout clothes, it was nothing compared to the life-threatening danger I encountered at the gym.

⌒

Before my Year of Transformation, the only time I'd been at a fitness class was at the Brewster-Wheeler Rec Center when Miss French got it in her head to teach "aerobics." She threw Rick James's "Superfreak" on the record player and led a handful of senior citizens in a soul train line with their walkers and canes. Then everyone headed outside for a smoke. In LA, working on your fitness is a lot more complicated.

The first class I tried at my neighborhood gym was something called "Beginner Yoga: Release and Relax." The first five minutes were delightful. The instructor, a dark-haired woman named Ursula, played soothing music and told us to inhale deeply.

"Feel the tension leave your body with each exhale," Ursula cooed in her melodic voice. She must have been an excellent teacher because I *did* feel the stress leaving my body. And then I felt something else: somebody was tapping on my shoulder. I opened my eyes to find a munchkin in yoga pants standing over me, her ponytail dangling in my face. "You are snoring *really* loud," she hissed. "It's messing with my chakras!"

Next, I tried "Thai Kick Boxing," which, as far as I could

tell, was a class of the same ass-whooping moves I saw angry mamas do every day at Brewster-Douglass.

After that, I signed up for a free session with Herby, a personal trainer at the gym. I liked Herby a lot. He was very flexible. But after only a few minutes, he cut our session short. Apparently, personal trainers don't like when you whip out your phone and start snapping close-up pics of their bulging ass muscles without asking.

The next time I went to the gym, I tried a class called "Disco Spin," which was advertised as a class "for anyone who loves a good beat." What the description failed to mention for those of us who hadn't heard of "spin" before was that all this music appreciation was supposed to happen while you were perched on top of a tiny stationary bike. When I walked into the room and saw all those bikes, I immediately turned around to leave. But the instructor leaned into her headset and called me out in front of everybody.

"Hey you!" she said, flashing a big smile. "There's a free bike over there." I cursed her under my breath as I made my way over to the unmanned bike she was pointing at and slid onto the seat. Everyone around me was peddling furiously. I started peddling, too.

Within seconds, I was so drenched in sweat it was like I'd been caught in a cat 5 storm surge. But I was keeping up! As the disco beat of the Bee Gees' "Staying Alive" came to an end, I raised my arms like Lance Armstrong crossing the finish line. I had survived the longest three minutes and fifty-six seconds of my life. I was so excited, I barely remember falling off the bike.

At the hospital a few hours later, a doctor shined a light in my eyes and told me I'd suffered a mild concussion. "We see these types of gym-related injuries a lot," he said. "You might want to take it easy."

All this time I'd been secretly thinking to myself that exercise might just kill me, and now this doctor was finally saying I was right. *Fuck going to the gym,* I thought. Those bikes weren't ready for all my jelly. It was time to change my weight-loss strategy. Instead of sweating my way to skinny, I decided to try dropping the weight the old-fashioned way—with a totally unscientific sounds-too-good-to-be-true crash diet.

For months, I tried every diet in the game: the soup diet, the grapefruit diet, the celery juice fast, and the cayenne and lemon juice cleanse. After spending my paycheck on grapefruits, protein shakes, and an expensive juicer, I did the "broke diet," that is when you don't have any money to eat.

One day in the Xerox lunchroom, my coworker Carol looked over at me as I was choking down a stack of rice cakes. Carol just shook her head. "Don't you remember when Oprah lost all that weight on Optifast?" she said.

Of course, I remembered! In 1988, while I was still in high school, Oprah's weight loss episode had been the television event of the year. For four months, Oprah had stayed on a liquid diet, drinking nothing but Optifast. She showed off her weight loss on her talk show, wearing her size 10 Calvin Klein skinny jeans and pulling a wagon filled with sixty-seven pounds of animal fat to illustrate how much she'd lost. I remember watching it one day after school thinking, *This is the whitest shit I've ever seen.*

"Look what happened to Oprah," Carol said. "She gained it all back."

Things You Should Never Say to a Curvy Woman

- "You gonna eat all that?"
- "I thought you were on a diet."
- "Leave some for the rest of us."
- "You remind me of someone....Oh yeah, the lady on the syrup bottle!"
- "Damn, you're pretty for a fat girl."
- "Are you having a boy or a girl?"
- "Can you give me a piggyback ride?"
- "You're not big big."
- "Does that dress come in regular people size?"
- "You'll never get married looking like that."
- "Oh Lord, you are huge!"

Carol had a point. Since embarking on my Year of Transformation, I'd tried fourteen different diets and lost a total of four pounds. After eating nothing but soup, grapefruits, or rice crackers all day, I'd treat myself to a couple—or three or four—Taco Bell Cheesy Gordita Crunches at night. Because I was hungry, dammit! At the rate I was going, my Year of Transformation was going to take a decade.

"There are all kinds of ways to lose weight and keep it off," Carol continued. I glanced over. She was eating a large bowl of what looked like weeds my granny used to pay me a dollar to pull out of her yard. "You might like Atkins or South Beach or Pritikin," she added, packing up her Tupperware. "You just need to find something that works for you."

I'd never heard of any of these diets before. But Carol got me wondering if maybe there was a better way. I decided I needed to do more research. After work I hit up my local bookstore in search of the perfect diet book to help me change my life. All these years later, I'm still thankful for what I found.

～

That evening, as I wandered the aisles of Barnes & Noble looking for the weight loss books, I found myself in the memoir section. My eyes landed on a copy of *The Autobiography of Malcolm X,* the book that Mr. Arnold told me had changed his life. I'd never finished the copy I'd been reading that day on the GM assembly line. I wondered what it was about the book that made such an impression on Mr. Arnold. I'd never read anything that had that kind of impact on me.

On the same shelf, I caught a glimpse of another memoir, *Secrets of the Sparrow* by Diana Ross. Like me, Diana Ross had grown up in Brewster-Douglass and graduated from Cass Tech high school. But she'd gone on to become a superstar, and one of the most glamorous women in the world. Curious, I picked up the book and started reading, right there in the store.

Diana wrote about growing up poor, the hard work it took for her to rise to fame, and the pressure she felt trying to live up to other people's expectations. Most important, she explained how she regained her power by fighting back against those demands. I was so captivated by her story that before long I'd forgotten why I'd come to the store. I purchased the book and left. A few days later, I was back for more. Suddenly, dieting wasn't the only thing on my mind. Over time, I hardly thought about it at all.

Over the next few months, I devoured books by Toni Morrison and Terry McMillan. I immersed myself in stories by, for, and about black women. I learned about the incredible accomplishments of a legion of sisters who'd come before me, from Hattie McDaniel, the first black woman to win an Oscar, to Mae Jemison, the first black woman to go to space. And I came to understand that the women I admired the most—from Moms Mabley to Oprah Winfrey—didn't gain success by conforming to other people's expectations or waiting to be invited to the party. They broke down barriers, stayed true to themselves, and became successful precisely because they *weren't* like everyone else. These queens showed me what was possible if only I stopped trying to change who I was just to get along. It was the greatest lesson of my life.

Of course, this is not to say that my Year of Transformation was a total success. Before I came to my senses, I wasted a whole lot of time. For almost an entire year, my career had gone nowhere. I was so focused on changing who I was that I didn't go onstage or to any auditions. I was so obsessed with losing weight I didn't spend any time working on my craft. Instead, I risked my life at the gym and wasted my money on one fad diet after another. In the end, I didn't lose any weight. All I lost was time.

I moved into the next year with a whole new mind-set. Instead of thinking of my full figure as a roadblock to my success, I decided to embrace my luscious curves and appreciate the opportunity I had to be a role model for other people who look like me. If I could pull this off, and become a success on my own big-booty terms, I would be a game-changer instead of just another person playing the game.

Hollywood didn't need another skinny girl, I decided. What the industry needed was somebody exactly like me.

Big Girls Rock: Top Reasons to Appreciate a Full-figured Woman

- Because I said so.
- You wanna fight me?
- I look good, dammit.
- When I twerk, it's a big deal.
- I'll keep ya warm in winter.
- I order great take-out.
- My breasts feel like sofa pillows.
- You'll always sleep in a king-sized bed.
- I'm easy to find in a crowd.
- When we walk together, people part like the Red Sea.
- I'm less likely to get snatched off the street by a predator.
- You'll never go hungry.

CHAPTER 12

ANYTHING CAN HAPPEN
ON THE WAY TO SUCCESS

In Hollywood, there is nothing more terrifying than your first "table read." That's when the whole cast of a TV show or movie sits around a giant rectangular table and reads through the script, with the director looking on and assessing everyone's performance. Often, the first time an actor does a table read it's in a low-stakes situation, like a student film. But the way things worked out for me, my first read-through was at the fancy-ass MGM Studios in Beverly Hills. I had been cast as "Shaniece," a bubbly airport security agent in the high-flying comedy *Soul Plane.* This was going to be my big break, my chance to show the whole world just how funny I could be. I figured if I killed it in *Soul Plane,* who knows what other opportunities would come my way.

I entered the rectangular-tabled room and looked around, trying to find my name on the cards placed in front of each seat. Like most read-throughs the head of the table was reserved for the director, Jessy Terrero, and the stars of the film: Kevin Hart, who was on the come-up at the time, Snoop Dogg, Method

Man, and Tom Arnold, who everyone knew from *Roseanne*. I was seated near the middle of the table, not far from Sofia Vergara, who was playing a sexy stewardess, and beside the woman with whom I would share a few hilarious scenes, one of my favorite comedians, Mo'Nique.

I'd never met Mo'Nique in person, but I'd watched her plenty of times on *The Parkers,* and I knew she was an excellent actress. What intimidated me even more is that I'd also seen Mo'Nique do stand-up a few years earlier, at the Just for Laughs comedy festival in Montreal.

Just for Laughs is the biggest comedy festival in the world, with hundreds of comics performing at showcases all over the city. I wasn't performing though. I'd gone to the festival to study the craft, get inspired, and catch up on industry gossip, because I'm nosey like that.

The show I was most excited to see was New Faces, which features stand-up comedians who haven't yet made it big. In the industry, getting picked to perform at New Faces is a *huge* deal. Agents, network executives, and bookers fill the audience and a good set can kick off a career. The year I attended, Mo'Nique was showcasing with Craig Robinson and Niecy Nash. Niecy was hilarious, and so was Craig, who played keyboards during his set. But it was Mo'Nique who stole the show.

She strutted onstage in a majestic gold and black floor-length gown with a train in the back and an Elvis Presley popped collar that fanned out and framed her face. I'd never seen anyone perform with such confidence and don't-give-a-damn attitude. Plus, she was unapologetically raw. It takes a lot of lady balls to dress like royalty and cuss like a dude who just lost his child support case, but Mo'Nique pulled it off.

Now here I was at my very first table read for my very first film slipping into a chair beside her. I was so nervous all I could think was, *What if I mess up? What if she doesn't think I'm funny? What if she throws her lady balls at me?*

With my heart beating out of my chest, I introduced myself and told Mo'Nique I was excited about working with her. I will be forever grateful for what she did next. Mo'Nique leaned in close. "Let me give you some advice, sis," she whispered. "Just do it exactly how you did at your audition. This is no time to be shy."

I followed her advice and read my lines like my life depended on it. The whole room erupted in laughter. Mo'Nique nudged me gently. Under the table, so no one else could see, she gave me two big thumbs-up. I couldn't stop smiling. All my hard work was finally paying off.

⁓

It had been three years since I'd given up on my pursuit of skinniness in favor of embracing the curves God gave me. For all that time, I'd been on my grind, focusing on my career. I hit up every spot on the LA Chitlin Circuit and started going out on the road, too, opening for other comics in clubs across the country. Most important, I started making moves to get myself stage time at some of the big mainstream clubs in Hollywood, like the Laugh Factory on Sunset Boulevard.

It seemed like every comic who ever got a TV deal had played the Factory, from Bob Saget and Ray Romano to Chris Rock and Dave Chappelle. Compared to the venues where I was used to performing—like the back of Roscoe's Chicken and Waffles, which might seat about fifty people, max—the Laugh Factory held more than three hundred and felt enormous. The problem was, I couldn't just go up to the club's owner, Jamie Masada, and ask him for some stage time. I had to jump through all kinds of hoops before he'd give me a chance.

Every Tuesday at ten a.m., the Laugh Factory would post outside the club a sign-up sheet for an open mic. The first twenty comics to get their names on the list were allowed to do a three-minute set in front of a live audience later that night. Jamie would watch the performances, and if he thought a comic was good enough, he might make them a "regular." At the Laugh Factory, being a regular meant Jamie would give you stage time every week. It might be a ten- or fifteen-minute spot on Wednesdays or a standing gig to emcee a show. Either way, you'd get the chance to perform in front of hundreds of people, and, because it was Hollywood, someone important— like an agent or TV booker—might be in the audience. To a comic, exposure is everything. For years, becoming a Laugh Factory regular was my number-one goal.

On Tuesdays, those twenty open mic spots filled up quick. To have a shot, comics would start lining up outside the club at the crack of dawn, with lawn chairs. Once you put your name on the list, you had to stick around all day to make sure another comic didn't scribble out your name and add their own—because comics are desperate like that. At the time, I was still holding down my full-time job at Xerox. So, every few months, I'd call out sick from work with the flu, or an earache, or a stomach virus, or a touch of the Ebola, and take my ass to Sunset and wait in line for hours just to get my name on the list.

For almost three years, every time I performed, Jamie would tell me the same thing: Come back in six months and try again.

Each time Jamie told me I wasn't good enough I'd spend a few days feeling crushed. Then I'd pick myself up and get back on my grind, trying to get stage time wherever I could. Eventually, I landed a regular gig working as the weekend emcee at the Annex, the seventy-seat room inside the Ice House, a big mainstream club out in Pasadena.

People think that all an emcee does is introduce the next act. But emceeing at a comedy club is way more complicated than simply bringing people onstage. It's like foreplay with someone who's not in the mood—it's a lot of work!

At a comedy club, when the audience first arrives, folks are usually stone cold sober, and maybe some of them are even coming in straight from a stressful day at work. They are stiff and tight-lipped and not in a prime laughing mood. That's what you call a "cold room." Comics hate that. An emcee's job is to warm up the audience by getting folks loosened up and ready to laugh. A room can also go "cold" later in the night. Let's say a comic goes up and bombs, it would be my job to turn the energy back up before the next comic came onstage.

At the Ice House, I'd try all the wildest things I could think of to get the audience warm. Sometimes, I talked in different voices. One time I came onstage singing Aretha Franklin. Another time I tried to pop and lock and popped my ass right off the stage. But soon enough, I got the hang of crowd foreplay—I'd talk a little, tell them what a great audience they were, make a few jokes, and leave them wanting more.

Between weekend emceeing at the Ice House and the hours of stage time I put in on the Chitlin Circuit, by the time I got up for Jamie at the Laugh Factory one Tuesday night in the fall of 2002, I felt comfortable and confident.

Onstage, I did a tight three-minute set and when I was done, I got a standing O. It had taken me three years of trying, but I'd nailed it! After the show, I approached Jamie with an ultimatum. "If you don't make me a regular tonight," I said, "I'm never coming back."

Jamie stared at me for so long I began to worry that I'd stepped way outta line. But then, he smiled. "You killed it," he said. "Come back tomorrow."

That's how I became the Factory's Wednesday night emcee. Jamie paid me seventy-five dollars a show. Not only did I get a chance to do a few minutes of my own material every Wednesday night, I also got to see a lot of heavy hitters like Dave Chappelle, Richard Lewis, and Damon Wayans perform. I studied the way these guys worked the room, managed hecklers, and built joke after joke on a single premise. I remember on my first night watching from the balcony thinking to myself, *I gotta get my shit together and elevate my game.* I was sharing the stage with comedy greats, but still I wanted more.

⌒

You never know when someone who irritates the hell outta you is going to end up changing your life. That's what happened to me the day Bob, the Eddie Murphy–impersonating comedy fan I worked with at Xerox, came sprinting toward my desk. Ever since I'd started at Xerox, I tried to stay clear of Bob. It

Things to Do at Work Instead of Working

- Update your résumé
- Bookmark pornhub pages to watch later
- Flirt with your coworkers
- Find a place to take a nap
- Install a margarita machine in the break room
- Hack into the office server to find out if your boss really has a college degree

wasn't just the offensive Eddie impressions. It was also the way Bob would try to sound "urban" and slang it up whenever he talked to me.

"Yo," he said, leaning over the wall of my cubicle one fateful day. "Whadup, homie?"

"I'm fine, Bob, and I'm not your homie."

"My bad, Nubian Queen," he said with a grin. "But check it: I've got the four-one-one on some dope-ass comedy bizizzle."

I sighed. "I'm kind of busy right now," I said. I was in the middle of designing a circuit board for a new line of photocopier, and I didn't have time to chitchat with Bob.

"For real, though!" he insisted. "My homeboy who does

stand-up told me about an open call. Don't sleep, Loni. You need to get on this fa shizzle."

Bob gestured toward my computer. "You mind?" he asked, with his fingers poised above my keyboard. In fact, I *did* mind. But I also wanted Bob to leave me the hell alone, and I figured letting him show me whatever he wanted on the computer might be the quickest way to get him to go.

"Sure," I said, rolling my chair back to give him room. Bob did a quick search and pulled up what he was looking for: a press announcement from HBO saying the company was holding auditions for a spot on their New Faces showcase at the US Comedy Arts Festival in Aspen. The showcase was to feature twenty up-and-coming acts, but most of the comics who performed at the festival were established enough to have managers who helped them get on the bill. So, HBO was also holding open castings—one in New York and one in LA—to find two undiscovered comedians to fill out the show.

"Thanks, Bob," I said, impressed with his info. "This *does* look good." To show my appreciation, I gave Bob a fist bump and made his wanna-be-down day.

The US Comedy Arts Festival doesn't exist anymore, but in 2003 it was a big deal. It featured all kinds of comedy, from stand-up to feature films. Getting selected from an open call was a long shot, to say the least. But you can't hit it big if you don't even try.

The next day, I called in sick to work. "I think I have swine flu," I told my boss, coughing into the phone. Then I drove over to a nightclub at Universal CityWalk to line up with more than six hundred other hopefuls to perform my ninety-second set.

I made it through the first round and was called back, along with thirty other comics, to perform later that week at the Hollywood Improv on Melrose Avenue. We were told we'd be performing six minutes in front of a live audience and a handful of HBO execs who would make the final pick.

I walked into the club and looked around. The place seated two hundred, but the only people in the room were the row of HBO execs sitting in the back, the comics waiting to perform, and a handful of audience members sprinkled throughout the club. The place felt empty.

I watched the comics who went up before me with a sinking feeling in the pit of my stomach. Onstage, comic after comic was going straight into the set they had prepared and all of them were bombing, hard. When my name was called, I knew I had to do something different. Just then, all my training as an emcee warming up ice-cold rooms kicked in.

"Damn," I said, looking around. "If this is for HBO, I'm going over to Showtime!" From the back of the room I could hear the row of executives howling. With that one line, I'd turned the room.

I did six minutes about cubicle life and some new material I'd been working on about sending my cousin Skillet to track down terrorist Osama bin Laden and left the Improv feeling good about my set. The execs must have liked what they saw because out of hundreds of comics they picked me! Three months later I was on my way to Aspen.

Aspen is one of the coldest and most snow-covered places I've ever been, but the minute I hit that town, it was on fire. Not only did I kill during my set at the New Faces showcase, after my performance the festival organizers invited me to appear on a few other showcases, including "Women with Attitude," one of the biggest draws at the festival. I'd be sharing the bill with Nora Dunn from *Saturday Night Live,* stand-up Lynne Koplitz, and headliner Janeane Garofalo, who was famous for her political humor. I was a huge fan of Janeane, and the idea of sharing the stage with her intimidated the hell out of me. I was an unknown comic and she had her own stand-up special on HBO.

Backstage before the show, I tried to act casual, but I was nervous as hell. The ballroom at the St. Regis Aspen Resort held almost a thousand people and was filled with movie stars, talent agents, and executives from every major studio. Kelsey Grammer, who was hosting the show, was hanging out backstage, along with *Sex and the City*'s Kim Cattrall and comedian David Alan Grier. I was the only comic on the bill who didn't have a manager, so when Janeane and Kelsey started talking about the lineup for the show, I didn't have anyone to advocate for me. All I could do was listen and nod, like whatever they were saying was okay with me.

Janeane told Kelsey that her act was going to be kind of heavy and might bring down the audience. "Loni should go after me," she said.

"Okay," he replied. "We'll have Loni close."

I kept a smile plastered on my face, but I was freaking out. Nobody wants to follow a comic who cools down the room. Plus, I was the least experienced of all the performers. I was the *last* person who should close the show. That was the headliner spot, it's supposed to be reserved for the most famous comic on the lineup. The closer is when audiences expect to get the biggest laughs. It felt like I was getting thrown in the deep end before I could swim. But what could I do? Janeane was a star and I was a nobody. I had no choice but to go along.

Sure enough, Janeane hit the stage and launched into a heated political rant. She talked about the war in Iraq, President Bush, and the terrorist attacks of 9/11. It wasn't that she didn't get laughs—of course she did, she's a pro—but like she'd predicted, her act made people uncomfortable and you could feel the energy leave the room. It reminded me of that scene from *Coming to America* where Randy Watson and his band Sexual Chocolate perform a passionate version of Whitney Houston's "Greatest Love of All" to a packed auditorium and only four people clap.

After Janeane left the stage, Kelsey Grammer didn't even try to bring back the room. He just shrugged and said, "And now, Loni Love."

Then I walked onstage.

I looked out at the crowd, gripping the mic with shaking hands. I noticed Mike Myers sitting in the front row, staring at me expectantly. My mind cast back to all the comics I'd seen at the Factory who'd been able to turn a room with nothing but swagger and confidence. And I remembered my auditions. Turning a room is how I got to Aspen in the first place! Once again, it was time to show what I could do.

"This show is called 'Women with Attitude,'" I began. "I don't know why y'all got me out here," I paused and looked around, taking a beat. "Because I DON'T HAVE A FUCK-ING ATTITUDE!" That one line, delivered with just the right energy and commitment, was exactly what the audience needed. Over-the-top attitude hit the audience just right. The sound of a thousand people erupting in laughter was the sweetest thing I've ever heard. They didn't stop laughing until I left the stage.

Looking back on that night all these years later, I have so much appreciation for Janeane. At the time, I didn't think I had the skills to close a big show. But Janeane thought different. Instead of closing the show herself, she gave me a shot and let me shine. I'll always love her for that. Like I always say, great things happen when women have each other's backs.

After the "Women with Attitude" showcase, my life began to change in ways I'd wished for so many years. *Variety* magazine called me one of the most talked-about stand-ups in Aspen that year, and at the gala awards ceremony that closed the festival, David Alan Grier presented the Jury Prize for Best Stand-up to me. The week before, not a single industry bigwig had ever heard of Loni Love, and now folks were saying I was one of the best comics in the game. It just goes to show you, if you put in the work grinding your ass off year after year after year after year, you, too, can become an overnight sensation.

~

For almost two years after the festival, my life was a whirlwind. Not only did I get a manager, the great Judi Marmel, and sign my first network development deal with HBO, I also appeared on CBS's *Star Search* revival hosted by Arsenio Hall.

I competed in the stand-up comedian category against a bunch of men. The winner was supposed to get a $100,000 prize and a development deal with CBS to possibly create their own show. Even though I was the only comic to get a perfect score from all the judges, I ended up losing in the final round.

But still, *Star Search* got me in front of a lot of viewers, which I was grateful for. As Judi told me, there are only two reasons to take a job in Hollywood: to make money or to be seen. Exposure leads to new opportunities, she said. And she was right.

A few months after I appeared on *Star Search,* I got cast as Shaniece in *Soul Plane.* And if all that wasn't enough, that year I also fulfilled my original acting dream of appearing in the sitcom *Girlfriends.* If you're a superfan of the show, you might remember me from the "New York Bound" episode. I played the part of "Woman." Yes, that's right, my character wasn't important enough to have a name. But I didn't care, my real name was in the show credits. That's all that mattered to me.

Things were going so well, I started wondering if maybe it was time for me to quit my job at Xerox to pursue my dreams full-time. But the idea of giving up a regular paycheck and a dental plan scared me to death. That's when God sent me a sign.

The higher-ups at Xerox announced they were making company-wide layoffs. I told my boss to let me go and save someone else's job. He raised his eyebrows like I was crazy, but I assured him I would be alright. After all, I was getting industry opportunities left and right. What could possibly go wrong?

❦

It turns out the most important thing to know about making it in Hollywood is that nothing ever turns out like you planned. You can hustle and strive and work your ass off and plan for the future and make vision boards and to-do lists and set your eyes on the prize and then, when you least expect it, everything can

What NOT to Do After a Career Setback

- Kidnap your (former) boss
- Mail dog poop to the HR department
- Sleep with random coworkers one at a time or as a group
- Run away with the circus
- Rant about it on social media

blow up in your face and you're back to square one. I know because that's exactly what happened to me.

When I auditioned for *Star Search,* I was required to sign a "holding deal" with CBS as a condition for being on the show. The holding deal wasn't going to give me any money, but it did mean I was locked down and couldn't work with any other studios. Holding deals aren't as exciting as development deals, which is when a studio says they are interested in developing a project with you attached. Still, signing that deal with CBS felt like I was taking my first step to something big. CBS was home to *King of Queens* and *Everybody Loves Raymond.* The network loved giving comedians their own sitcoms.

I signed the deal with CBS in February 2003, a month before I appeared at the US Comedy Arts Festival in Aspen. In March, after I won best stand-up at the festival, HBO—home to some of the best shows in television history—offered me an actual development deal. I couldn't believe it! Even though there were hardly any black women starring in sitcoms at the time, I was going to get a chance. Lying in bed one night, I marveled at the turn my life had suddenly taken. It felt too good to be true. And it was.

I quickly discovered that contractually I couldn't take the HBO deal while I was in a holding deal with CBS. But because I didn't win *Star Search,* CBS wasn't going to give me a development deal, either. Instead of getting my own show, I ended up in limbo. It's sort of like if you married your high school sweetheart, Tony, and then on the way home from the wedding Tony gets hit by a bus and goes into a coma. Then, the next day, you meet Dwayne "The Rock" Johnson in the cookie aisle of your local grocery store, and he says, "You're hot. How about I take you to Vegas for the weekend?" Now what are you going to do? You can't say yes to The Rock because you're married to Tony. Only Tony's in a coma and he can't do shit for you.

I needed to get out of my situation with CBS so I could run off to Vegas with HBO, but I didn't know how.

In the end, I had to get a lawyer. Most attorneys wouldn't take a case like mine—I didn't have money to pay them; I was a Hollywood charity case. Eventually entertainment lawyer Jamie Mandelbaum took pity on me and got me out of the CBS deal for only a 5 percent commission.

Finally, I was able to move forward with HBO. The studio paired me with an experienced TV showrunner who was supposed to help me come up with show ideas, but this middle-aged white guy and I were not a good fit. He thought I should play a teacher in a public school. My idea was for me to star in a black *Sex and the City,* only this time the city would be Detroit, and instead of my character having a closet full of designer shoes, I'd have a cupboard full of stuff I bought at the ninety-nine-cent store. We ended up pitching the showrunner's idea to a few major networks. Nobody took the bait. I remember one executive looking me dead in the eye and saying, "You don't fit here." In the end, like so many other Hollywood development deals, my HBO deal fizzled out.

But at least I had my career-changing breakout role in *Soul Plane,* right? Well, that didn't work out the way I'd thought it would either. In case you're too young to remember, in 2003 there were two ways to watch movies: in theaters or on DVDs at home. Typically, a Hollywood film would be available on DVD a few months after its theatrical release. DVDs sold for about thirty dollars back then, which was hella expensive. That's why so many people went the illegal route. They bought pirated copies of their favorite film from some guy selling bootleg DVDs on a street corner.

I don't know how things are where you live, but in cities like New York, LA, and Detroit, making and selling pirated DVDs was the hustle. Enterprising dudes would set up folding tables on the sidewalk and hawk DVDs that they'd copied from real DVDs for half the retail price. Where bootleggers really cornered the market was when they came out with a DVD version of a movie that was currently playing in theaters, months before the official DVD went on sale. But these DVDs were the worst quality you can imagine. Knuckleheads would make them by smuggling VCR cameras into movie theaters and taping movies as they played on the screen. Sometimes you could even see the backs of people's heads sitting in the theater's front rows.

Even so, if you were on a budget, buying a five-dollar street copy of *Freddy Versus Jason* and popping some popcorn on the stove was a whole lot cheaper than paying for two full-price movie tickets and snacks at the concession stand. Bootleg DVDs were the original Netflix and chill.

Soul Plane got the bootleg DVD treatment, too. Only we got it worst of all. Somehow some shady-ass character got a copy of the *original* master of the film six months before it was scheduled to hit the theaters. It was the earliest any illegally copied movie had ever been available on the streets. In fact, months before *Soul Plane* was scheduled to open in theaters across the country, the FBI raided a bootlegging operation in Philly and confiscated fifteen thousand pirated DVDs. The only movie in the collection that hadn't already played in theaters was *Soul Plane*. By the time the movie opened on Memorial Day, everyone had already seen it.

When D. L. Hughley, who plays an in-flight bathroom attendant in *Soul Plane,* went on *Jimmy Kimmel Live!* to promote the flick, Jimmy said, "It looks like it's a funny movie. In fact, I should have seen it already because we've had this bootleg of *Soul Plane* here for three weeks."

Without missing a beat, D. L. replied, "I had it while we were shooting the movie."

To fully understand how devastating this was, you have to remember that, back then, the only thing that mattered to movie executives was box office sales. Our opening weekend ticket sales were a disaster.

Soul Plane was supposed to be my big break. And although it did eventually turn into a cult classic, the movie did so badly at the box office, in the industry it was considered a major dud.

And ain't nobody trying to cast you in another movie if you just came off a flop.

I felt like all my hopes and dreams were crashing down around me. It was like having sex with a really bad lover. I had started out really excited, expecting fireworks, only to end up frustrated, and curled up in bed alone, nursing a bottle of Hennessy and a tube of Pringles. Which is exactly how I spent the summer of 2004.

All those years I'd spent busting my ass, driving all over town to perform midnight sets at comedy clubs, while holding down a full-time job at Xerox—and what did I have to show for it? I had no steady income, no TV deal, and no movie career. I didn't even have a dental plan anymore. For weeks, I was so low. I felt like a failure. But late one night, curled up in bed with my Hennessy and barbeque chips, I had one of those sudden realizations that makes you wonder why you never thought of it before: *Maybe I felt so shitty because I was focusing on the wrong things.*

For years, I'd been hustling to make connections and get exposure because in Hollywood fame is how everybody measures success. But when had fame become my goal?

I thought back to my happiest memories: the feeling of exploding fireworks I had onstage at the rec center, the joy when Mo'Nique flashed me a thumbs-up under the table, the rush of satisfaction when the audience erupted in laughs at Aspen. Those thrills are the reason I became a comic in the first place. I was in this industry because I love entertaining. Becoming rich and famous wasn't ever my goal, yet here I was making it the measure of my success. I'd forgotten my first love and instead was judging myself by criteria I didn't create or care about. That's why I felt so low.

That night, I made a vow to myself to change my perspective and think differently about the opportunities that came my way. Of course, I had to pay the rent and I needed industry execs and fans to see me shine, but there is more to life, happiness, and feeling fulfilled than money and fame. I also needed to feed my soul. I promised myself to say yes to opportunities that sparked my interest and joy even if they didn't meet the industry criteria for success. And I'm so glad I did. Changing my perspective led me to one of the most exciting moments of my career.

Do you know what the china pattern on the coffee cups in the White House looks like? Well, I do! Yes, that's right, y'all, your girl Loni Love from Brewster-Douglass Housing Projects has had the pleasure of enjoying a cup of coffee with the best president of the twenty-first century, Mr. Barack Obama. And how did I get this chance of a lifetime? Not by landing an HBO development deal or by starring in a blockbuster movie. I got my special invite because I followed my heart.

In 2008, I became cohost, along with rapper MC Lyte and radio veteran Angelique Perrin, of *Café Mocha,* a syndicated radio program aimed at women of color. The brainchild of broadcasting veteran Sheila Eldridge, *Café Mocha* was going to be hosted and produced exclusively by black women— something that had never been done before. When I first signed on to do the show, Sheila didn't have a single station that had agreed to air it. All she had was an idea: on *Café Mocha* we were going to interview celebrities and tackle important political and social issues, like gun violence, drug sentencing laws, and voting rights, all from a black woman's perspective. The job offered very little pay and an uncertain future; as a syndicated show, there was no guarantee we'd be picked up anywhere. But I believed in Sheila's vision, and I wanted to be involved. To me, taking the chance to speak to women about our concerns and entertain them in the process felt like I was answering a higher calling.

As *Café Mocha* launched, Sheila hustled more and more syndication deals, and it quickly became the most-listened-to radio program for women of color in the country. We interviewed not only A-list celebrity guests, like Aretha Franklin and Jennifer Hudson, but also game-changing politicians, like Maxine Waters, and activists, like Sybrina Fulton, Trayvon Martin's mother, who was on a mission to keep other young black men from being brutally murdered like her son had been. It was the reach and impact of *Café Mocha* that led me to the White House.

On August 4, 2012, President Obama, who happened to be celebrating his birthday, invited a handful of African American radio personalities to the White House to talk about the upcoming midterm elections and ways we could encourage our listeners to get out and vote. I went, repping *Café Mocha*.

It took all kinds of self-control for me to hold back my tears as I walked up the path toward the towering front doors of the West Wing. A white-gloved Marine sentry watched me as I approached, perfectly timing his movements so that he'd open the door just as I was ready to enter. "Thank you," I whispered as I passed. He looked so serious I wasn't sure if I was supposed to speak to him.

Inside the foyer, a secretary checked me in and pointed

toward the waiting area. Reverend Al Sharpton and gospel singer Yolanda Adams were already there. Yolanda and I had never met in person before, but we were both so overcome with emotion we immediately started hugging.

Before the meeting, we were told that we'd be allowed to ask President Obama one question each. When it got to my turn, I started by complimenting the president on passing the Affordable Care Act. "I know so many people are happy because they can finally go see a doctor and check their rooter to the tooter," I said. President Obama let out a chuckle. Then I asked what initiatives he thought would help black women—who make sixty-one cents to every dollar earned by white men—receive equal pay. I wish I could remember his answer, but the minute he smiled at me and said, "Well, Loni...," I fell into a daze. All I could think was, *President Obama just said my name!*

Before we left the meeting, I gave the president a birthday present. I admit, April Ryan gave me the idea. She stood up, wished Obama a happy birthday, and handed him a card. I'd brought along a copy of my first book, *Love Him or Leave Him, but Don't Get Stuck with the Tab.* As soon as April returned to her seat, I saw my chance. I sprinted to the head of the table. "Mr. President," I said. "This is for you. Happy birthday." Roland Martin started laughing and told me to sit back down. But the president said I was okay and asked the White House photographer to snap a pic of the two of us. I never did get a copy of that photo. But somewhere in the historical records of this great nation of ours is a picture of the president of the United States holding a copy of my dating advice book. Standing right beside the president is me, Loni Love from Brewster-Douglass Housing Projects, grinning like a fool.

Sometimes life takes unexpected twists and turns. Although the path to success can be filled with disappointments, there are also good surprises along the way. My advice to anyone struggling with career or life choices is, try to say yes to opportunities that replenish your spirit as much as your wallet. Life is unpredictable. But your heart will always lead you right where you need to go.

CHAPTER 13

REAL TALK

"I want my own show," I told my manager Judi over the phone. There was a long silence on the other end of the line, like she was drawing a breath that she would never finish. "I know," she finally said, "but this could be a good opportunity, Loni. It will get you in front of the right people. You know how this works."

I sighed long and deep. For more than a decade—ever since I'd quit my day job at Xerox—I'd been hustling nonstop and paying my dues. I'd played every stand-up club that would book me and pursued every TV opportunity that came my way.

Do you remember those talking head shows that used to be real popular in the early 2000s, where they'd show a clip and then cut to a comedian cracking a joke about said clip? Yeah, I did *all* those shows. Like every single one, including *I Love the 70s, I Love the 80s, I Love the 90s, I Love the 80s Strikes Back,* and *I Love the 90s Part Deux*. I appeared in ninety-four episodes of truTV's *World's Dumbest* and did *Hollywood Squares, Premium Blend, The World Dog Awards,* and *World's Funniest Fails*. I was a comic for hire, which is a little like being a call girl, except for less pay, and I got to keep my clothes on.

Eventually, I started getting invites to do guest appearances on daytime talk shows and nighttime roundtables. I was a regular on *Rachael Ray* and appeared on *Chelsea Lately* more than a hundred times. But as much fun as I was having chitchatting about my love of bacon and day drinking, I craved something more. I wanted a chance to control the content and create my own show. Sometimes, I would lie on my sofa with my tube of Pringles and fantasize about doing an hour-long variety show that featured sketch comedy and musical guests, like *The Carol Burnett Show* or *The Jacksons,* programs I'd loved as a kid. But I knew I'd never get that kind of opportunity until I proved myself. So, I kept on grinding.

By 2010, my career was beginning to gather momentum. I'd recorded an hour-long stand-up special, *America's Sweetheart,* for Comedy Central. Not long after that, Ellen DeGeneres invited me to be a guest DJ on her talk show. This was a huge deal. Ellen had one of the most popular programs on daytime TV, and the two of us really hit it off.

Ellen liked to quiz me about my dating life on air, and she even started sending me out to do field segments. One time I took a pole dancing class. Another time she had me go to Fairy Princess school, where I learned how to entertain kids at birthday parties. To Ellen's amusement, I dressed up in a purple gown and silver tiara and scared the shit out of a bunch of seven-year-old girls. As a comic, you have to put yourself out there because you never know when someone important is going to see you shine.

During one of my *Ellen* appearances, I got spotted by Hilary

Estey McLoughlin, the production president at Telepictures. She'd been watching the taping from the booth and had commented out loud, "I don't know why Loni doesn't have her own show. She's hilarious." A production assistant who'd overheard Hilary passed the compliment on to me. That was all I needed to hear. I called my manager and asked her to arrange a meeting with the Telepic exec.

In the industry, these meetings are called "generals." A general is when a talent (say, a comedian, screenwriter, or director) and a bunch of execs get together to feel each other out. As the talent, it was my job to get the executives excited about the prospect of working with me. A general is like the worst parts of a job interview and a first date, but without the free dinner.

The first thing I noticed when my manager Judi and I walked into Hilary's Burbank office was that nobody was smiling. That room was as cold as the meat freezer at Ralphs. I swallowed hard and started talking. I told them about my childhood in Detroit, my win at the rec center talent show, and my dreams of hosting a variety show. They must have liked what they heard because I walked away from that meeting with a Telepictures development deal.

Of course, I knew from my experience with HBO that development deals don't always lead to shows. Even so, I felt a ray of hope. This was the opportunity I'd been dreaming of, a chance to create something that would be all mine. If Telepictures wasn't interested in a variety hour, I thought maybe I could do a sitcom. I had a bunch of ideas I was excited to pitch. Like, I could play the first black woman president of the United States who is secretly having an affair with her press secretary, played by Idris Elba; or I could play the mayor of a small town who is secretly having an affair with the city comptroller, played by Idris Elba; or I could play a checkout clerk at Albertsons secretly having an affair with Idris Elba. The possibilities were endless.

I signed my development deal in the fall of 2015. Now, here I was a few months later, with Judi on the other end of the phone telling me that Telepictures wanted me to audition for a project they had in the works, one that did not involve Idris Elba at all. "This has nothing to do with your development deal," she explained. "It's for a talk show they are planning, with four or five women cohosts."

"They already got shows like that on the air," I countered. "Why would I do something that's already being done?"

Judi said Telepictures was planning a different type of talk show, aimed at a younger demographic. Plus, all the hosts would be women of color. "It's something completely new," she said. I was intrigued. But still, cohosting a talk show wasn't what I'd signed up for. I wanted my own show.

Judi and I went back and forth until we finally came up with a compromise: the producers of this new talk show were having a chemistry read, meaning they were going to try out different combinations of prospective hosts. I agreed to participate in the auditions, but only as a "placeholder." As a comedian with lots of TV experience, I knew I could be helpful getting the conversations going during the audition. The way my manager described it, I was doing Telepictures a favor. And besides, she pointed out, you don't say no to the same producers you hope will one day give you your own show. This was an opportunity for me to show the higher-ups at Telepictures I was a team player.

A few weeks later, I went to the chemistry read for *The Real* fully resolved in my mind that I wasn't going to do the show. At least, that's what I thought at the time.

～

I arrived at the Telepictures studios in Glendale on a bright March day. A production assistant led me to a room with a large round table. Off to the side were three cameramen, a showrunner, and a bunch of execs huddled around a TV monitor.

Seated at the table was a woman I knew had already been cast in the show. I could see why Telepictures wanted her. She was charismatic, outspoken, and hella sassy with the kind of big personality that plays well on the small screen. We smiled and introduced ourselves and then the showrunner called in three other women to join us.

As the cameras rolled, the showrunner fed us hot topics to discuss, like: Should all couples sign prenuptial agreements? Is it okay to send naked pictures to a man you are dating? How did the election of the first black president impact your view of politics? Every so often, the showrunner would interrupt the conversation, pull one woman out, and bring in someone new. In all, we cycled through dozens of women that day, including former child stars, other comedians, a bunch of women I'd seen in reality shows, and a few I didn't recognize at all.

You can really tell a lot about a person when you seat them at a table full of strangers and encourage them to talk. Some people are nervous babblers, saying a whole lotta nothing, and others immediately light up the room. And then there are the people who bring magic to any conversation, like Adrienne

Houghton, who is more bubbly than a glass of Champagne; and the fearless Jeannie Mai, who says the kind of stuff most people just keep in their heads while looking as glamorous as a supermodel; and Tamera Mowry-Housley, who is warm and thoughtful and the kind of person who would know exactly what to do if your kitchen curtains caught on fire while you were making grilled cheese.

During the auditions, I was surprised that so many of the women at the table were married or in serious relationships. Whenever the showrunner asked us to discuss dating life, I made sure to represent for the single and satisfied contingent. When the other women at the table said they didn't think sending naked pictures was a good idea, I piped up, "That's because you ladies haven't seen the pics dudes send in return. Some of my text threads look like a urologist's scrapbook!"

I left the chemistry read feeling good that I'd done my part and played along, and now I could go back to dreaming up scenarios for my sex scenes with Idris or ideas for the *Loni Love Variety Show* sponsored by Popeyes. But my daydreaming didn't last long.

A few days after the auditions, my manager let me know the folks at Telepictures thought I'd done so well at the chemistry read, they wanted me to sign on for the show. One of the producers called me himself. He insisted *The Real* would fill a void, speaking not only to young women and women of color but also to women in middle America who would benefit from hearing different perspectives. "*The Real* is going to be groundbreaking," he said. The producer also promised I'd be able to pursue my own show on the side. "We'll only tape three days a week," he assured me. "You'll have plenty of time for other projects."

I had to admit I loved the concept. Between Los Angeles and New York, there is a whole world of people who've never had a black friend. I thought it would be a great public service to show middle America that women of color are more than the stereotypes they may have learned. Plus, if the chemistry read was any indication, I knew working with Jeannie, Adrienne, and Tamera Mowry-Housley—or her twin; I wasn't sure which one I'd auditioned with—would definitely be a whole lotta fun. In the end, the decision was easy. How could I possibly say no?

The Real premiered with a four-week test run in a handful of Fox markets in the summer of 2013 and went into full syndication the following year. By 2015, we were the top-rated daytime talk show for the coveted eighteen- to thirty-four-year-old demographic. If fans weren't watching us on TV, they were catching up on social media. We have the biggest social media following of all the roundtable talk shows on the air.

Fans love *The Real* because we aren't like any other show. We decided early on that nothing would be off-limits and our "Girl Chat" segment features some of the most brutally honest convos you'll see anywhere on TV. Sometimes we even surprise ourselves. None of my cohosts knew about the miscarriage I had when I was in my twenties until I talked about it on the show and broke down in tears. And Adrienne, Tam, and I were stunned when Jeannie told us on air that she'd spent two months in federal prison. We start conversations on topics other shows are afraid to touch, and share the good, the bad, and the ugly to let our fans know that whatever struggle they are facing they aren't alone.

On *The Real,* we also cover news of the day from a perspective you don't usually see on daytime TV. We had the first televised interview with Rachel Dolezal, the former president of the Spokane chapter of the NAACP, who claimed to be a black woman when, in fact, she was white. Our thirty-minute segment made headlines because, unlike other media, we felt comfortable asking Rachel to explain what in the name of Black Baby Jesus she thought she was doing. We also featured a shocking interview with Jerhonda Pace, one of R. Kelly's sexual abuse victims, years before the Lifetime documentary *Surviving R. Kelly* brought the R & B star's predatory behavior to the attention of mainstream America. We addressed school shootings, childhood trauma, and spilled all kinds of tea.

More than anything, we aim to uplift and elevate our fans and encourage them to love themselves the way they are. Where else on daytime TV are you going to see women of color encouraging each other to celebrate their natural hair and love their full-figure curves? We knew our show was revolutionary, but we never imagined that five years in, we'd also be recognized for our accomplishments, winning two NAACP Image Awards and a Daytime Emmy. But of course, in television as in life, no matter how great things appear on the surface, all kinds of drama were surging beneath.

~

Okay. I'm going to be all the way real about this. The last thing I feel like doing is rehashing the situation with the original cast member who left the show in 2016. But because it's something that fans of the show are always asking me about, I'll give you my side of the story. I'm not dishing dirt or spilling tea. I'm just telling you the truth about what happened and how it impacted me.

The first I heard about the cast changeup was on Saturday, May 21. I was in New Brunswick, New Jersey, where I was performing at the Stress Factory as part of my "Funny Kind of Love" comedy tour. Sometimes people ask me why I still go on the road when I have a full-time job on TV. Stand-up is my first love. I'll never stop wanting to get up close and personal with an audience. It's the best way to make folks laugh. Just you wait, one day you're going to see a senior citizen Loni Love pushing a walker onstage, talking about getting some of that good-good nursing home sex.

I love going on the road, but it can be exhausting. That's why I follow a very strict napping routine. I like to get a solid two-hour snooze in before I hit the stage. So, on this particular Saturday afternoon, I was in my hotel room drifting off to sleep when my phone rang with an 818 number that I recognized as coming from Telepictures. I couldn't imagine who it could be. We'd finished taping the second season of *The Real* the month before, in April, and we weren't scheduled to return to set until the end of August. We were on hiatus and there was no reason anyone from the show should be calling.

"Hello?" I said, propping myself up in the bed.

On the other end of the line was one of the show's executive producers telling me that one of the cast members wouldn't be returning in the fall.

I was stunned. I thought back to a few weeks earlier when we'd wrapped the show. There had been a photo shoot with all five of the hosts. None of the producers had made any indication they were even *thinking* of changing the lineup. In fact, all five of us were scheduled to appear at the Essence Music Festival in July.

"But wait," I said, grabbing my glasses off the nightstand, suddenly wide awake. "Can we talk about this?"

The producer told me that the decision had already been made. "But why?" I pressed. "What happened?"

I was told this was between the cast member and the producers, which is Hollywood speak for "none of your damn business." Telepictures and the ousted cohost were going to make public announcements, I was told. It was a done deal. There was nothing more to discuss.

I hung up the phone and felt my heart sink. None of this made any sense. I quickly glanced down at my phone and checked social media to see if there were any reports about the shake-up. I was stunned by what I saw. The woman who'd just been let go had posted on Instagram that she'd just been "stabbed in the back." Then she unfollowed me.

The next few days were chaotic. I tried to reach out to the cast member, as did the other women on the show, but I never got a response. I even posted a heartfelt video to Facebook expressing my care and concern. One of our sisters had been put out and I wanted her to know she wasn't alone. "She helped build this show," I said. "I am so sorry this is happening. It's very confusing for all of us." I posted the video without asking permission from the studio execs and as soon as they caught wind of it, they contacted my manager Judi and made it clear that I was not to discuss the issue any further. For years, I didn't say a word. But while I stayed silent, folks on Black Twitter wouldn't stop talking.

Internet sleuthing fans of the show quickly discovered that the former cohost had unfollowed me as soon as she'd posted her angry Instagram comment about feeling betrayed. They assumed I was behind the firing. I became the focus of thousands of online attacks.

They went after me on Twitter, Facebook, and Instagram and shaded me on podcasts. People posted hateful rants about me on YouTube and set up phony Twitter accounts for the sole purpose of calling me a lying, two-faced, fat, jealous bitch. Someone edited my Wikipedia page to include that I was responsible for my cohost being fired. I was bullied and fat shamed and called every ugly name in the book. Twitter trolls even sent me death threats. It got so bad that for a few weeks I had to make my Instagram account private. As a comedian, social media is how I communicate with my fans and let people know about my upcoming shows; it's how I sell tickets. The online harassment was weighing on my spirit, impacting my livelihood, and making me feel unsafe.

Of course, talk shows change their on-air talent all the time. Since its 1997 debut, *The View* has had twenty-two different cohosts. The only woman who has been there since the beginning is Joy Behar. Anybody who works in television knows that getting let go is part of the game. But like any game, this one has rules. Number one: no matter what's going on behind the scenes, in public you behave like a professional. That's why you don't see Tamron Hall, Sherri Shepherd, Megyn Kelly, and Ann Curry—who all lost high-profile jobs on prime-time TV— on social media reposting insults about their former coworkers. That's not how it's done.

I wish I could tell you that the insults and bullying didn't get to me because I am a strong woman and I've survived worse. I wish I could say I let it all roll off my back. But the truth is it hurt. A lot. On social media, people can be so cruel, saying things they'd never say to your face. It's hard not to take it personally when people are calling you a lying bitch and holding you responsible for a situation over which you have no control. Plus, the accusations didn't even make sense. If I really did possess the power to hire and fire and change the direction of a show, I'd use that clout to have my own damn sitcom.

When I was getting attacked on social media I felt totally alone. People I thought were my friends did not stand by me; people who knew the truth didn't come to my defense. In some ways, it reminded me of how I felt when my mama kicked me out. I was getting blamed for something I didn't do and cast out into the cold. Except for a few close friends in the industry, I didn't tell anyone how much I was hurting. All I could do was stand in my truth and know that I'd done no wrong.

All this chaos went down in the summer of 2016. If you've followed the story, you know it didn't end there. In the fall of 2019, the situation was back in the news when the former cohost took to social media and, again, accused me of orchestrating the plot to get her fired. But this time there was a very different reaction.

Instead of getting mass attacked on Twitter and Instagram, I got an outpouring of support. Fans, friends, and industry peers wrote, saying they appreciate me and know I'm not to blame. They called me classy and honest and sent me lots of love. The reaction was different this time around because three years had passed since the initial scandal and viewers had come to know me even more. They'd seen me stand up for sisters and cry real tears over stories of other people done wrong. This time they weren't so easily fooled by false accusations. I have worked for more than a decade in this industry trying to get ahead. I have never—not once—tried to advance my career by pushing another woman down. After three years of being in public, on TV, or on social media almost every day, I didn't have to convince anyone of my intentions. Everybody can see the truth.

I feel horrible that this ugliness has become part of the story of *The Real*. The show is supposed to be a celebration of our diversity and a place for women to come together. That we've had to spend even a second engaged in pettiness and name-calling hurts my heart. But, like I always say, in every struggle there is a lesson. This professional challenge taught me one I'll remember forever: no matter how hard they come for you, if you stand in your truth and behave with integrity, no one can take you down.

Job Interview: Things to Ask Before You Say Yes to That New Position

- Does the vending machine have Skittles?
- Can I nap at my desk, or do I need to nap underneath it?
- Do you really expect me to be here at nine every day?
- Can I get an advance on my first paycheck?
- How long are the breaks?
- How many chances do I get to pass the drug test?
- Exactly how many single and handsome men work here?
- Does Arbor Day count as a paid holiday?

CHAPTER 14

NEVER TOO LATE FOR LOVE

"No one should go through something like this alone," my good friend Yvette Nicole Brown said, comforting me during one of our late-night phone calls. It was the summer of 2016, during the height of the online attacks directed at me after the nasty shake-up at *The Real*. I was feeling especially low; Yvette was one of the few people I could lean on.

You probably know Yvette as Shirley Bennett from *Community,* or Helen Dubois from *Drake and Josh,* or as a superfan of *The Walking Dead*. The two of us have been close for more than a decade. We'd met at a fancy end-of-the-summer barbeque at casting director Robi Reed's house. Robi is a legend in the industry. She's the one who cast Halle Berry in her breakout role in *Jungle Fever* and put Denzel in *Mo' Better Blues*. I landed an invite to her star-studded soiree because Robi was also the casting director of *Girlfriends*. Taking that small walk-on role as "Woman" in season 4, episode 23 really paid off!

As soon as I walked into Robi's beautiful home, I caught sight of Yvette sitting alone on a bench by the pool. I recognized her from the auditions circuit and went to join her. We were both so new to the industry, neither of us knew anyone at the party. We spent the day together, enjoying the glamour that surrounded us and sharing stories of castings gone wrong, and building our sisters-in-the-industry bond.

I met a lot of black women back in the day, at auditions and comedy clubs when we were all starting out. Tiffany Haddish, Leslie Jones, Sheryl Underwood, Octavia Spencer, and I all ran in the same circles. We'd compare notes about which shows were casting black folks, and how we could get ahead without having to play the "sassy best friend," a prostitute, or a maid. In other words, we were talking about the struggles of being black in Hollywood a decade before #OscarsSoWhite trended Twitter.

Of course, it wasn't all bad. We had a lot to celebrate over those years, too. If one of us landed a high-profile gig, it felt like we'd all had a win. And not just because we were happy for each other, either. It turns out that a lot of white folks could not tell us apart. So, when Octavia starred in *The Help,* people would come up to me in the cookie aisle at the supermarket to tell me what a great job I'd done.

Of all the sisters I met coming up, Yvette and I were especially close. We supported each other through our ups and downs and had a standing appointment to watch the Emmys, Grammys, and Academy Awards together over the phone. When Mo'Nique, Octavia, and Viola won their Oscars, I celebrated in my apartment, with Yvette screaming on the other end of the line. Naturally, when things took a turn during those months of online bullying, Yvette was the one friend I leaned on the most.

"You know I'm here for you," Yvette said that evening while we talked on the phone. I'd just finished telling her about a death threat I'd received over Instagram and she could tell I was feeling overwhelmed and a little scared. "But I wish you had a partner at a time like this," she continued. "Someone to hold you down and be there for you so you wouldn't have to go through this alone."

As I lay in bed later that night, I thought a lot about what Yvette had said. I began to wonder if maybe she had a point.

For more than two decades, I had been living life completely on my own terms. I did everything for myself, by myself, and just the way I liked it—from planning my own birthday celebrations to managing my own money. If I wanted to blow a paycheck on some fancy bacon and top-shelf brown liquor, that was my business. On *The Real,* when all the other ladies were talking about their married lives and sharing their booed-up perspective, I proudly represented for the happily single women of the world. I know there are women out there who have dreamed about getting married since they were little. But that just wasn't me. Maybe it was the memory of how my mama doted on Tyrone that turned me off. Or maybe it was my independent spirit. All I know is that finding a serious partner wasn't high on my priority list. I enjoyed being solo when my life was in control. But facing a challenge like online bullying made me feel very much alone.

～

I haven't always been single. There was a time, not long after I broke up with Lavar—the man who wanted to make me into a black Stepford wife—that I briefly experimented with the marriage lifestyle.

Johnny and I met a few months after I decided to leave my engineering job at Xerox to pursue comedy full-time, in the spring of 2004. I was performing stand-up for the troops in Hawaii. After the show, a short, dark, and handsome soldier approached me to say how much he enjoyed my set. He explained he was stationed in Hawaii but on leave for the week, and he asked if I'd like to join him for a drink. I usually don't socialize with men I meet after shows, but I was in Hawaii, and everybody knows what you do when you're in a different time zone doesn't count.

Johnny and I spent the next four days together, enjoying candlelit dinners and long walks on the beach. We looked like a couple from a Viagra commercial, only we weren't having sex. We just talked and talked. When I returned to Los Angeles, we quickly started a long-distance relationship, spending hours on the phone and racking up frequent flyer miles traveling between LA and Hawaii to see each other. The whole thing was crazy romantic and totally unrealistic. Just like most LDRs, we fell in love with the voice on the other end of the line, but neither one of us had to make any compromises in our day-to-day lives like you do in a real relationship, which suited me just fine.

We'd been seeing each other for almost two years when Johnny told me that for his next leave, he wanted us to meet in Las Vegas. I love playing slots, so of course I said yes. It turns out Johnny wanted me to take a way bigger gamble.

As I pulled up to the Vegas address where Johnny had told me to meet him, I discovered it wasn't a hotel; it was the Clark County Courthouse. Johnny was there on bended knee, holding a dozen roses. "Will you marry me?" he asked with a grin.

I was so shocked, I blurted out the first thing that came to my mind: "I have to pee!"

I darted past Johnny and headed inside the courthouse to the ladies' room to try to collect my thoughts. Marriage is not something I'd thought of before. But I *did* love Johnny, and he'd gone to all this trouble. Plus, he was fine as hell. I exited the ladies' room and found my man standing by the door still holding the bouquet. I gave him a big hug. "Let's do this!" I said.

Getting married so suddenly was like living out a scene from a romantic comedy. But it didn't take long before reality hit. A few months after we got hitched, Johnny got assigned to a base in North Carolina, and he expected me to move there and live with him. But I just couldn't take the plunge.

My career was finally taking off. I feared that if I left LA, everything I'd been working for would have been for nothing. Being a wife just wasn't worth giving up on my dreams. Plus, it wouldn't have been fair to Johnny to have me as a lifelong partner: I didn't want kids; I like to get drunk in the mornings; and my preferred sleep position is spread-eagle in the middle of the bed.

To his credit, Johnny took it well. We went our separate ways, but we've stayed friends to this day.

My short-lived marriage to Johnny helped me clarify my priorities. After the divorce, I focused all my attention on my career and reserved dating for something I dabbled in on the side. Relationships were too time-consuming and distracting to let myself get caught up. Lucky for me, getting caught up wasn't a problem. None of my flings ever had a chance of turning into anything real because my dating strategy was to never let a man know the real me. I was a master of dating under false pretenses.

Let me explain: I'm a woman with very specific likes, dislikes, and ways I get things done. I love to eat but I don't like to cook. I'm a hard worker, but I need frequent naps. I like kids, but not in my house. I get invited to a lot of industry parties, but my idea of a good time is watching *All About Eve* on Turner Classic Movies while eating Pringles out of the can. That's the reality of who I am. But there's not a single guy I dated who knew any of that.

For years, whenever I started seeing someone, my MO was always the same. Instead of being up-front about my likes, dislikes, and sex position preferences, I'd bend over backward to accommodate the man. I was that "cool chick" who went along to sporting events, hip-hop concerts, Super Bowl tailgating parties, MMA cage matches, and illegal dogfights if that's what my man was into. I would go along to get along, all the while getting more and more irritated, until I suddenly had enough. Then I'd end the relationship because he was too...*whatever,* and move on to the next. It was a cycle I'd fallen into without even realizing it. In the end, it took a sex-related injury for me to finally see the light.

I'd been dating this guy who was way too young for me. He was so young I should have ended the flirtation the minute he sat down beside me at a bar and asked to buy me a drink. I should have said, "Why don't you take your hairless chest and your skinny jeans and go find someone your own age to play with?" But instead, I found myself staring at his smile, dazzled by his beauty, and going along for the ride.

Terrance and I ended up dating for a couple of months. To this day, it was the most stressful relationship I've ever had. I was a grown-ass woman, but Terrance was living that twenty-something life. He shared an apartment with four of his fraternity brothers and he slept on the lower level of a bunk bed.

Leave the Young Boys Alone! Reasons Not to Date Younger Men

- They cry if you get mad at them.
- You have to carry their juice box in your purse.
- You can't buy them nice clothes because they are "still growing."
- They have a curfew.
- You have to buy their drinks at the club.
- If you hurt their feelings their mamas will fight you.

Worst of all, we weren't even sexually compatible. As an adult, I prefer Anita Baker–type sex—slow and easy. But Terrance was barely out of puberty. He had the stamina and flexibility of a Cirque du Soleil performer. There was no way I could keep up. The first time we got busy, Terrance threw some crazy-ass trap music on his JVL speakers, climbed on top of me, and started churning my legs like an eggbeater.

"Time out!" I yelled. "Young man, my body do not move like that!"

Suddenly, I heard a loud crack. At first I thought it was the sound of the bunk bed frame coming apart, but as I learned in the ER later that night, it was my L6 vertebra. That's what you get for dating outside your fitness level.

After that, I slowed my roll when it came to dating. I made a commitment to stop wasting time with men who were too young, too athletic, too into sports, too broke, too into their healthy lifestyles, and *definitely* those who were too into their mama's cooking.

By the time I started working on *The Real,* the only thing that was hot and heavy in my life was me after I'd finished a thirty-minute speed walk on the treadmill. Instead of wasting my time on go-nowhere relationships, I was focusing 100 percent on myself, my career, and my happiness. I had a lot of time to reflect.

On *The Real,* I talked a lot about being single and satisfied. I was proud of my independent status. But deep down, I began to wonder why I'd made this particular life choice. *Why was I so satisfied alone?*

The truth hit me late one night as I was drifting off to sleep. I thought of my mother and the way she'd pushed me out of her house for the affection of a highlighting fool, and I was suddenly overcome with a hurt I'd never felt before. That's when it hit me: When you get rejected by your mama—the one person in the world who is supposed to love you unconditionally—it leaves a wound that's hard to heal. It dawned on me that all my life I'd been guarding my heart and protecting myself.

Instead of letting men see who I really was, I'd date dudes I knew weren't great matches for me, and then, when it didn't work out, I could tell myself it was all his fault for being too into sports, or cars, or healthy eating.

Even if the dude was the one who called it quits, I didn't feel the sting of rejection because he wasn't rejecting *me*—the authentic Loni—he was breaking up with some crazy woman who was pretending to like tofu.

All that fakeness was the perfect setup to never get hurt. But it was also the perfect setup to never find real love.

When I got off the phone with Yvette late that night. I couldn't stop thinking about what it might be like to have a companion in my life. Not just any guy, but a real partner who would be there when things got rough and hold me down when I felt scared and alone.

I knew if I was going to find a real partner, I needed to change things up. No more pretending that I liked watching football or doing gymnastics in bed. I was going to bring the real Loni to the table. If I was going to invite someone new into my life, this time I was going to do it right.

$\backsim$

I don't know how I managed to be single for so long without ever taking part in the pleasures of online dating. Call me old-fashioned, but I thought the best way to meet guys was in bars, where you can evaluate important details, like if he has crazy eyes or keeps his money held together by a rubber band. But when Yvette told me I could use a dating app to meet cute guys all while lounging at home in my sweats and no bra, I was sold.

Yvette explained that all I needed to create an online dating profile were a few cute pictures of myself. I immediately started scrolling through my photos looking for the perfect pics. As an entertainer, I have all kinds of professional headshots, but in my new mission to put my true self out there, I decided I'd only use selfies.

I settled on what I thought were three excellent pics. The

first was a bedroom selfie. Only mine wasn't one of those sultry photos where a woman is half-naked, peeking out from under her bedsheets. My selfie is what I like to call "early morning realness." I snapped it at the crack of dawn when one of my eyes was still swollen shut. The other pic was a bathroom selfie I took in the locker room at my gym after a brisk speed walk on the treadmill. I was drenched in sweat and in the background of the photo you can see the bottom half of a naked senior citizen drying off her feet. The third snap was me in the cookie aisle at the grocery store giving a thumbs-up in front of the Oreo Double Stuffs display.

Yvette also told me I needed to include a little info about myself, so along with the photos I put my age, height, and weight, and "I like bacon, naps, and brown liquor." Satisfied that my profile captured the real me, I posted it on one of the more popular dating apps, then waited for a match.

Loni Love's Online Dating Profiles Demystified

What's in his profile:	What he wants you to think:	What it really means:
A picture of himself with a tiger	He's brave	He's been to the zoo
A picture of himself with a young child and the caption "Not my kid!"	He's good with kids, but doesn't have one	That's his kid, and he's only allowed supervised visits
"I love long walks"	He's romantic	He doesn't own a car

What's in his profile:	What he wants you to think:	What it really means:
A picture of himself beside a woman with a scribbled-out face	He's not a loser. He has female friends.	Stay away. She might be tied up in his basement.
A picture of himself at the gym looking hella swole	He works out and has the hard body to prove it	He knows how to use Photoshop and that is not his body
"I'm not into game playing"	He's being real with you	He's married with five kids
A picture of himself behind the wheel of a late-model Benz	He's rich and drives a nice car	He works part-time as a valet
A picture of himself holding a fist full of 100-dollar bills	He's a baller!	He was arrested shortly after that picture was taken
"Let's go for coffee"	He wants to get to know you	He only has three dollars

I got a hit right away. His name was "Tim." His first message to me read, "I'm a personal trainer. I'd be happy to work with you. I'll even give you a discount. You look like you need help."

Fuck you, Tim.

The rest of the guys I matched with that evening weren't any better. "Kevin" was into big-game hunting, "Roger" said he was already married and hoped that wouldn't be a problem, and "Karl" sent me a bunch of eggplant emojis and said he could be over in thirty minutes if I paid for his Uber.

Obviously, I was doing this all wrong. I opened my profile

and took a long hard look. Maybe in my quest to be real, I'd overcorrected. Maybe letting people see you first thing in the morning or sweaty at the gym isn't the best way to attract the kind of man I was looking for. I took down my profile and created a new one, this time with a picture of myself flashing a big smile. I typed, "No kids but love family. Kind and caring. Love a guy with a sense of humor. No married dudes, please." Within a few weeks, I was talking on the regular with two men who couldn't be more different.

Marcus was a really sweet and talented musician. On our first date, he invited me to a church service where he was playing organ. I felt all eyes on me when I walked in and took a seat.

I get it. People were buzzing because it's not every day that the lady you watch on daytime TV shows up at Sunday worship. After the service, an usher approached me. I thought he was showing me the way out, but instead he led me to the pastor's office. The minister had written a book, he said, and he wanted to know how he could get it mentioned on *The Real*. I tried not to hold this press-hungry pastor against Marcus. But it reminded me that dating as a celebrity comes with its own special challenges.

The other dude I was talking to didn't watch daytime TV and didn't know who the hell I was. The first thing James said to me when we matched on the dating app is "I like your smile." I responded that I liked his eyes, which were warm and friendly. James and I texted back and forth for a few weeks and then I promoted him to actual phone calls. James told me he was an actor and also owned his own painting business. *He's a grown-up who's got his shit together*, I thought. But then, not long after we started talking, he ghosted me. I didn't hear from him for two weeks. I tried not to get too salty about it. But deep down, I was insulted. I thought we were getting along!

Then out of nowhere, James called me again, like nothing had happened. I tried to act casual, but I had to know the truth. "Where have you been the last thirteen days, eleven hours, and thirty-eight minutes?" I asked.

James seemed genuinely confused: "Has it been that long?" He'd been busy at work, he explained, and hadn't even noticed the time go by. "It's not that I'm not interested," he said. "That's not it at all."

I know a lot of women who would have kicked him to the curb right then and there. Nobody likes when a guy disappears without warning. In fact, when I told Adrienne about getting ghosted during a "Girl Chat" segment on *The Real,* she freaked out. "I'm shocked and almost appalled," she gasped. "I think James is such a good guy, but now you are making me reconsider things!" I love Adrienne, but I thank God she isn't my dating advisor.

To me, the keys to successful dating are to get to know a person before you make any rash decisions and to trust your instincts. As a busy person myself, I know what it's like to get caught up with work. And it's not like we had sex and *then* he disappeared—we hadn't even met in person. Plus, getting busy at work is a way better reason to not call someone than other excuses I've heard. I have a friend who dated a guy for three months and suddenly he stopped returning her texts. When he finally reached out to her weeks later, he explained he'd been busy binge watching all nine seasons of *The Office.* My friend ended up marrying this dude and they're living happily ever after with two kids and a dog.

My point is, people do all kinds of stupid shit at the beginning of relationships. If you're going to have a zero-tolerance policy and take everything as an insult, you're never going to get anywhere with anyone. James seemed sincere when he explained why I hadn't heard from him. I decided to give him a second chance and I'm glad I did.

After our initial misunderstanding, James really stepped up. He started calling or texting me every day before I went to work just to let me know he was thinking of me. I get up at four-thirty in the morning. I figured he was setting his alarm just to give me a "have a great day" call. That's what I call commitment. Eventually, I lost interest in dating anyone else. I began to focus all my energy on James.

One Friday night after I'd had a particularly stressful week at work, James picked me up, drove out to the Pacific Coast Highway, and parked by the side of the road overlooking the ocean. He put some Rod Stewart on his car stereo, which I promptly switched to Aretha, and we sat together watching the sun go down. I've never had a nicer evening.

Another time, about three months after we started dating, the brilliant conductor Roderick Cox invited me to his debut performance with the LA Philharmonic Orchestra at the Walt Disney Concert Hall. I'd met Roderick on Instagram. Like me, he got his start playing the French horn. Roderick also happens to be a brother. As a big fan of classical music, I was thrilled to get the invite. In the past, I'd always gone to these kinds of events by myself. I've seen Misty Copeland and *Hamilton* and visited the Getty Museum alone. It's not that I like going solo, it's just that the guys I dated always found classical music, ballet, and the theater a nerdy bridge too far. I figured James would feel the same. But I asked him anyway. "I don't suppose you want to come with me to this concert, do you?"

To my surprise, he said he'd love to. James looked so handsome the night of the concert, suited up and freshly shaved. I couldn't take my eyes off him.

It's hard to pinpoint the exact moment you fall in love with someone. I think when you're older, love happens more like a slow burn than a sudden explosion. But still, I'll never forget the moment I looked over at James as we sat in the concert hall, his face lit up with enjoyment as the sounds of the orchestra washed over us. He squeezed my hand and without taking his eyes from the stage he lifted it to his lips and kissed my fingers. I felt like my heart would burst.

James and I have been together for more than a year as I write this. We've spent vacations together and long lazy Sunday afternoons relaxing on the couch. I like his gentle smile and his little quirks, like the way he never cusses and instead shouts, "Shut the front door!" or "Jiminy Cricket!" when he gets angry, which always makes me laugh. Most of all, I love the way he makes me feel like no matter what I'm going through he's there to support me.

Of course, James is different from the men I've dated before. He's closer to my age, he has grown children, and he's a white guy, which I used to think would mean a lot, but so far the only difference I've noticed is that now there's a jar of mayonnaise in my fridge. Of course, there are the haters and assholes online who called me a "sellout" and a "bed wench," which is one of the ugliest names you can call a black woman. One man even created a thirty-minute YouTube diatribe comparing me to a slave and James to a plantation-owning white devil. I called my attorney right away. I'm not sure what lawyer strings he pulled, but the video isn't there anymore. I'm from Detroit; if you mess with me or my man, I'm comin' for ya.

I've heard people say James and I make sense together because "opposites attract." But our relationship isn't successful because we're so different. It's because I finally allowed a man to see who I am with all my "faults" and in all my glory—he knew what he was getting into and he still stuck around.

James has never asked me to change or mentioned my weight or complained about the number of days I am on the road doing comedy; instead, he calls and checks up on me whenever I'm away. He's even seen me without my wig, which is a big deal for me—not because I think there is anything wrong with my natural hair but because underneath my wigs, I keep my hair in cornrows. Seeing your woman looking like she got her hair done on cell block C of the federal penitentiary can be a shock for a man if he's not expecting it.

A few months after we started seeing each other, James and I went to the Bahamas for a vacation. The resort we stayed at had a place where you could jump off a cliff and into the ocean. The two of us took the plunge. I hit the water and popped back up, but my wig had left my head and was floating off in the other direction. I was mortified. The only other time a guy I was dating had seen me without my wig on was when a dude took me on a roller coaster and a giant gust of wind blew the hair right off my head. And it was the last time I ever saw that guy.

As I watched my wig float away, I considered swimming after it. But then I thought better: *This is me in all my prison braids realness. James is going to have to accept me as I am.* I stood up in the water with my hands on my hips like Wonder Woman. "I lost my damn wig!" I announced.

James just laughed. "I think you look beautiful," he said. Then he swam off to retrieve my hair. I appreciate the hell out of James for that because wigs ain't cheap!

Ladies, take my advice, if you find yourself a man willing to brave an undertow to bring you back the hair you paid good money for, he's a keeper.

⌒

I've been doing stand-up almost all of my adult life and after every show I like to spend some time talking to my fans. You'd be amazed how many people line up just to ask me for relationship advice. People want to know how to meet someone special or how to get their significant other to stop being a liar or a cheat. Since I started dating James, the relationship questions have come at me like an avalanche. I get hit up on social media, after shows, and in the cookie aisle at the grocery store by people who are searching for happiness by finding somebody else.

I always tell people the same thing: If you want a partner, you deserve to have someone good in your life. Someone who holds you down during the tough times and laughs with you when the going is good. But no relationships will bring you happiness unless you are good with yourself first. The relationship I have now is a success *because* I did a lot of hard work before James and I ever met. I battled it out as a French horn–playing nerd, a ten-year-old entrepreneur, a broke-ass college student, a black woman in corporate America, and a sister trying to make it in show business. I've spent decades pushing back against the expectations people placed on me based on what I look like, and I stopped trying to conform. Instead, I embraced my "flaws" and celebrated my full-figured, nap-taking, wig-wearing self. Now that I've fallen in love with myself, I'm learning how good it feels to be loved by someone else.

So, the message of my story is simple. If you're struggling to change because you think it might bring you love, success, and happiness, maybe it's time you started thinking another way. Maybe instead of trying to change, you'd be better off focusing your attention on loving yourself and letting other people see the *real* you in all your quirks and glory. Because honey, believe me, after years of struggling I've come to see the truth: sometimes we don't need to fix our "flaws" to get ahead or get happy.

Now your best friend, on the other hand...between you and me, that girl needs work! But that's a whole different book.

ACKNOWLEDGMENTS

I never thought I'd be an author and here I am with my second book! Won't HE do it?! But I didn't get these stories out on my own, so I want to thank everyone who helped make this book possible.

To Jeannine Amber, girl, you are a strong and phenomenal woman, with a true gift for listening and asking questions without judgment and with love. Thank you so much for using your talent to help me tell my story. Niko is lucky to have you.

To my love, James Welsh. You are my knight in shining armor. This book wouldn't have an ending if not for you! Love you, my dear.

To my mom, Frances, without you there would be no me. Thanks for giving me courage, strength, and curvy hips!

And a special thank-you goes to my girls Monique Swygert, Rose Brice, and especially Yvette Nicole Brown for their friendship, support, and encouragement.

To the best manager in the world, Judi Brown Marmel, thank you for sticking with the curvy chick all these years. Having you in my corner allowed me to make it in this industry without having to get on the casting couch. I can't thank you enough for your support. My vagina thanks you, too.

To David Lamb, thank you for your enthusiasm for this project and your most helpful feedback. I wanted to include more anal jokes, but I think you were right to take them out. And to Miss Brandi Bowls from United Talent Agency, thank you for making this deal happen. You really get me and I appreciate that.

Thank you to the entire team at Hachette Go, especially Michael Barrs, for working so hard to get the word out. Thanks also to production editor Cisca L. Schreefel and copyeditor, Christina Palaia. And thank you to my publicist Elizabeth Much, you are a diamond on my team. As well, thank you to Jamie Lobel and the rest of the crew at East2West Collective.

To my assistant Alex Hill, thank you for keeping me sane and on track with everything, especially on days when I had a hangover. And to Paige Asachika, my social media manager, thank you for your creativity and not posting cat videos on my social accounts.

To the Levity team: Rachel Williams (you rock, lady), Chase, Steven, and Erin, thank you for making me one of the top comics on the club circuit, encouraging me to do this book, and supporting me through the process. And to Chris Smith at ICM Partners, I love you.

To Donna, Lauren, Rachel at Telepics, thank you for believing in me and continuing to support my love of helping women; and to John, Leo, and especially Yna at Power and Twersky, thank you for listening to my dreams and for always doing your best to help them come true.

To the ladies at Café Mocha: Sheila, Angelique, and Yoyo,

thank you for surrounding me with love and good talk every weekend. To all my Sorors of Delta Sigma Theta, Inc., thank you all for the support!!

And last, but most certainly not least, the biggest thank you of all goes out to my wonderful and amazing fans! Have I ever told you how much I love those sweet and encouraging messages you send? How I love seeing your faces light up when I'm onstage? How I miss you on my days off and wish you were there to go grocery shopping with me? I appreciate each and every one of you. It's a privilege and an honor to make you laugh.